Mum,

Happy Birthday & a very

Thank you for your support.

This book will help you reminisce and look forward to the next visit.

Michael, Jo, Harriet and Georgina

21/1/99

THE ORIENTAL BANGKOK

ANDREAS AUGUSTIN
ANDREW WILLIAMSON
PHOTOGRAPHS BY
HEIMO AGA

Andreas Augustin

presents

The Oriental, Bangkok

in the series The Most Famous Hotels In The World

This book was written at The Oriental in Bangkok.

Very special thanks go to Kurt Wachtveitl, the General Manager of The Oriental, who made this book possible.

The deepest gratitude for their help and kindness to

Penny Wachtveitl, Melvin J J Robson, Norbert A Kostner, Dr Parichart J. Suksongkroh, Jonas A Schuermann, Noppawan Phahulrat, Rabieb Boonkuncheing, Virochana Mochachandra, Eric Rosser, Supatana Atorn-Phtai, Jørgen Kamstrup, Susanne Worsfold, Phenkhae Chattanont, Anne Arunie, Chaturong Siewsutha and Carola E Augustin.

We treasure lovely memories of the late Mimi Berlingieri who shared her favourite anecdotes with us. We thank Chamchan Bunnag for her valuable research and information. We are also especially grateful to Pornsri Luphaiboon who set new standards in the field of public relations and to Ankana Kalantananda who helped so much with all her golden memories.

We are very grateful to HSH Professor Prince Subhadradis Diskul for his kind advises concerning the history of the Kingdom and we thank Gavin Young for his advices.

Last but not least many thanks to all the others who have contributed so generously to this book and who are not mentioned by name.

Editor's assistant: Yasmin Nissen; Research assistant: Herta Tschurlovits; Scripts: Julie Zhou;

Producers: Harrison Dolittle, Werner Graser and Michael Patzal

Photographs:

Celebrities: Aniwat Aeulek and the hotel's archives

Contemporary Oriental Hotel photographs: Heimo Aga

Editors in charge: Cherry Chappell, Andrew Smith and Andrew Williamson

First edition: 2/1996; Second edition: 6/1996;

Third and revised edition: 3/1997, Fourth and revised edition 11/1998

There is a limited leather-bound edition available.

ISBN 981-00-1287-X

For more information about The Most Famous Hotels in the World please contact our club fax ++43-1-87 77 904, e-mail: info@famoushotels.org,

WWW.FAMOUSHOTELS.ORG

Friends of The Most Famous Hotels
Glasauergasse 36
1130 Vienna
Austria

Design: Ramazotti Michelangelo

The Wai *(right page)*

Nothing is more typical of Thailand than that charming and universal greeting, the 'wai'. Both hands are raised, palms joined, to a position lightly touching the body somewhere between the chest and forehead.

The person who is junior in age or social rank is the first one to give the 'wai'. The senior person immediately returns the greeting, usually by 'wai-ing' with the hands raised no higher than the chest.

ANDREAS AUGUSTIN

studied hotel management at the Castle of Klesheim, Salzburg. He became a journalist, editor and publisher. In 1986 he has taken up residence for three years at the Raffles Hotel in Singapore to study and to write about the region and the hotels of South East Asia. Researching the history of the Oriental took him over one year. He visited the archives of the world searching old photographs, travel reports, postcards, diaries and historic advertisements. Other titles by him include Raffles, The Peninsula in Hong Kong, Metropole in Hanoi as well as various other books on famous hotels and destinations.

ANDREW WILLIAMSON

read Modern History at St Anne's College in Oxford. As co-author he has researched and edited this book. He has written 'Thomas Cook and the Golden Age of Travel' and is co-author and editor of other books in the 'famous hotels' series, such as the Grand Hotel Europe in St Petersburg and The Metropole in Hanoi.

HEIMO AGA

His photographic works include cover stories for Travel & Leisure, Newsweek and The New York Times Magazine. For this series he took most of the photographs of this book, the Metropole in Hanoi and the Grand Hotel Europe in St Petersburg.

Contents

A Long-Lasting Tradition

Two Oriental bell boys carry the Royal portraits to a function room in the hotel. The regal spirit is always present. The Royal Palace and The Oriental have a long tradition going back to the great Monarch Chulalongkorn's first visit to the hotel in 1890.

Respect, Love and Care

are the three words that spring to mind in Thailand where Monarchy is concerned. The Thais have a great admiration for His Majesty, King Bhumibol Adulyadej and Her Majesty, Queen Sirikit.

Captured Tranquillity

Wat Phra Keo at the Royal Palace has always been a favourite target for photographers. Photography, by the way, is one of the preferred hobbies of the Royal family who take up this art at a very early age (left). HRH Chulalongkorn's children shared the love of technical innovations with their father. The present king is a gifted photographer, too.

Dawn in Mae Hong Son

The province capital of Mae Hong Son in the northwest of Thailand awakes to an early-morning mist. Here the climate is cooler. A perfect holiday retreat for the Thais coming from the South where (picture to the left) miles of sandy beaches tempt us to spend a dream-like holiday. The diversity of Thailand is truly remarkable. Just half an hour flight from the hustle of Bangkok you land in a perfect paradise, be it surrounded by mountains or at the sea.

SERVICE CENTER
CATHAY PACIFIC AIR WAYS
CHINA AIRLINES
KOREAN AIR
Thai International
Thai Airways
北
京
虎
骨
酒
8-20450

One Day in Bangkok

'Don't fix to many appointments on one single day!' is a good motto when doing business in Thailand. Traffic in Bangkok like in many other metropolises around the world has become a severe problem. The inset shows the city end of New Road a hundred years ago when an occasional Rickshaw passed by a horse drawn carriage.

The garden

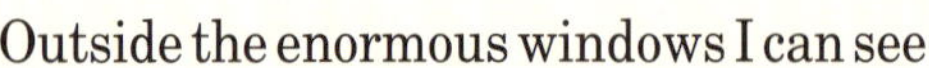

Traveller's Notepad

The pageboy bows with a smile. Slowly the doors swing shut behind me. A string quartet is playing Vivaldi's Four Seasons. Winter. At 30 degrees in the shade!

Outside the enormous windows I can see a corner of the pool. The first thing I always do is to walk right out to the front, to the terrace. Little tugs boars are towing strings of huge barges upriver.

Tomorrow, laden with rice, wood and other goods, they will be gliding past again, this time towards the Gulf of Thailand.

A visit to the famous Oriental Spa to counter my jet lag revives my spirits. How about a game of squash? Or tennis, perhaps?

The ballroom is magnificent. This is where famous artists like Peter Ustinov perform when in town. And José Carreras recently gave a concert on the terrace. Her Majesty the Queen of Thailand and an audience of 1,700 were knocked out.

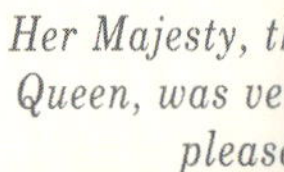

Her Majesty, t Queen, was ve pleas

The ball room

The duplex rooms of the Garden Wing exude a very special charm. If you are of a romantic nature, however, you may prefer the Authors' Wing, with its spacious writers' suites.

Pre traffic-jam days . . .

The Duplex Rooms

The two pools are an oasis at the heart of this bustling city. While the traffic comes to a complete standstill in the streets outside the Oriental, inside you find an atmosphere of tranquillity broken only by the hooting of the ships and the chugging of the long-tail boats.

At the pools

When night descends over Bangkok, the smell of charcoal hints at the magnificent buffets being served on the River Terrace. Lord Jim's upstairs serves the finest seafood in the city, and in the Normandie Grill you may find a visiting chef from one of the worlds finest restaurants demonstrating his culinary skills. The Sala Rim Nam across the river is Bangkok's most elegant Thai restaurant. And in the Bamboo Bar the jazz legends currently in town jam until the small hours.

Twice a day, the river changes its direction, due to the tides from the Gulf of Thailand in the nearby delta. Overlooking these mighty waters, my mind always wanders back to the day when Anna, the famous governess at the court of the King of Thailand, arrived. That was when the story of this hotel began, too.

Yin

is one of the two famous complementary principles of Chinese philosophy . . .

Yang

is the other one. Their interaction is thought to maintain the harmony of the Universe and to influence everything within it.

Siam in the late 19th century

WE BEG TO INVITE YOU TO OUR ROYAL PALACE . . .

On the right page the letter which King Mongkut sent to Singapore in 1862 to welcome Anna Leonowens as the governess of his children.

The English Governess Arrives

"English Era, 1862, 26th February
Grand Royal Palace, Bangkok.

"To Mrs. A. H. Leonowens:–

"Madam: We are in good pleasure, and satisfaction in heart, that you are in willingness to undertake the education of our beloved royal children. And we hope that in doing your education on us and on our children (whom English call inhabitants of benighted land) you will do your best endeavor for knowledge of English language, science and literature, and not for conversion to Christianity; as the followers of Buddha are mostly aware of the powerfulness of truth and virtue, as well as the followers of Christ, and are desirous to have facility of English language and literature, more than new religions.

"We beg to invite you to our royal palace to do your best endeavorment upon us and our children. We shall expect to see you here on return of Siamese steamer Chow Phya.

"Believe me
"Your faithfully,
"S.S.P.P. Maha Mongkut."

he red fireball sank majestically behind the huge monsoon clouds which paraded over the horizon like a herd of mighty white elephants.

A piece of land no larger than the captain's table floated gently past the Siamese steamer *Chao Phya* like a small green island. It must have made a long journey, torn from the bank of the Menam somewhere up north where the old capital Ayutthaya lay.

Anna watched it.

She sat down in the shade of the funnel. It had smoked busily ever since they stepped aboard in Singapore. She wore her hair up. Her feet were stuck in tiny, tightly laced boots. She folded her hands into her black skirt.

The steamer passed large expanses of betel-nut and coconut palms. On the other side were docks and shipyards. In the distance the golden peak of a huge temple loomed into the sky.

'They call these buildings pagodas here in Siam,' Anna thought.

The first houses, plainly built of brick and stucco, came into sight. One was flying the French flag. It was surrounded by plants and flowers.

'Mother?' A boy in a navy-blue seaman's outfit jumped over a pile of ropes and sat down next to Anna. 'Mother, is that Bangkok?'

'Yes, Louis. That is Bangkok.'

'And where is the king?'

Anna Leonowens smiled.

'I doubt that His Majesty himself will come to meet us, Louis. Don't forget to behave.'

The boy did not listen any more. 'Look mother,' he squeaked full of excitement, 'this *must* be the king!'

A long boat, adorned with beautiful golden ornaments, drew alongside. Wooden oars dipped into the water as the boat came to a stop next to the *Chao Phya*. A little gangplank was laid out and some of the passengers came on board of the steamer. Anna observed that they were greeted with great respect. Suddenly the captain of the *Chao Phya* waved excitedly at Anna.

'Look mother, this must *be the king!'*

'Mrs Leonowens! Mrs Leonowens!' He swiftly climbed the stairs to the upper deck. 'It is his Excellency, the Prime Minister Chao Phya Sri Suriyawongse. He has come to welcome you. A very great honour,' the captain explained.

Anna nervously stepped down.

'Welcome to the Kingdom of Siam, Mrs Leonowens.' Chao Phya Sri Suriyawongse greeted her with a deep bow. Then he scrutinised her from top to toe with a friendly smile. To Anna's eyes he was half naked. His torso was clearly visible.

'Thank you.' Anna looked round nervously. She was not used to talk to Prime Ministers. She tried to re-establish her self-confidence. At least she was the new governess of His Majesty, the king. His Majesty, Maha Mongkut himself, had sent a letter to her in Singapore: 'We beg to invite you to our royal palace to do your best endeavorment upon us and our children.'

He had also pointed out: 'You will do the best endeavor for knowledge of English language, science and literature, and not for conversion to Christianity; as the followers of Buddha are mostly aware of the powerfulness of truth and virtue, as well as the followers of Christ, and are desirous to have facility of English language and literature, more than new religions.'

Quintessentially English: Anna Leonowens. She arrived in Bangkok on 15 March 1862 and so become a legend.

'When will His Majesty receive us?' Anna asked.

'His Majesty, the king, will welcome you tomorrow morning.'

Anna shook her head in disbelief. 'Will we be sleeping in the palace?'

'I am sorry but we are not prepared for visitors. I fear it is too late today to make the necessary arrangements.'

'Didn't His Majesty . . .?'

Chao Phya Sri Suriyawongse smiled.

'His Majesty cannot remember everything. You can sleep wherever you want'.

'Where is there a nice hotel?' Anna asked.

'A hotel?' His Excellency looked surprised.

'What about all those buildings over there? That one looks like a boarding house.' She pointed at the building next to the one with the French flag.

'That is a seamen's lodge. Not quite the place for a lady to stay,' the captain informed her.

'What is the name of that place?'

'These oriental lodges are usually named after the owner, Mrs Leonowens,' the captain said, 'but please be my guest and stay for one more night on board. I will personally bring you to the palace tomorrow morning.'

'That's it then, isn't it.' Sri Suriyawongse ended the conversation. He bowed and with his men returned to their boat.

Six-year-old Louis Leonowens stood at the rail. His eyes followed the elegant barque as it slid majestically away. Small boats were passing by, flying flags showing a white elephant on a crimson background. Then his gaze fell on the small building next to the one with the French flag.

'Oriental lodge,' the captain had said.

'Oriental,' the boy murmured. 'Why couldn't we stay there?'

ORIENTA

OLD AND NEW

The commanding new River Wing built in 1976 overlooks the romantic original hotel dating back some 120 years. It is today playfully christened Author's Wing. The inset shows the same situation almost half a century ago.

'TO BUSINESS THAT WE LOVE WE RISE BETIME'

said Shakespeare as we will learn on page 136. Everything is done with a smile. The Oriental spirit is one of the many secrets that make this hotel so unique. While we continue our casual journey in this book through time and space all hands are on deck to prepare the various outlets of the hotel for new arrivals and old guests.

A white elephant!
Yes, these fabulous creatures really do exist.
Of course they are not the colour of pure driven snow, but rather a patchy light grey. But no one has any problem identifying white elephants. They have red eyes and five rather than four toes on each of their feet. They are sacred animals and it was considered highly auspicious if one was discovered during the reign of a monarch. The more that were found the better the portents for a successful reign.
The elephants, once found, were taken in great ceremony to Bangkok where they were placed in the royal stables and pampered for the rest of their lives.

The LAND *of the* WHITE ELEPHANT

A Historical Synopsis

he appointment of an English governess to the court in the middle of the last century was a clear sign of the opening of the kingdom to the West. It led automatically to an increase in foreign trade and a subsequent demand for proper hotel accommodation. The romantic element was that Louis' eyes fell lovingly on the building which was to become the country's most famous hotel. Over 30 years later he would become personally involved in the hotel's biography.

The Thai people came originally from south-eastern China. In the 10th century AD they began to migrate southwards and westwards and settled in the Indochinese peninsula. During the 13th century Sukothai became the first capital of an independent Thai kingdom. It was superseded in the 14th century by a new Thai state with its capital further south at Ayutthaya. For the next 400 years Ayutthaya flourished. The Siamese kings, absolute rulers of their people, patronised the arts and dedicated huge temples to Buddha.

The history of this period is littered with the names and dates of an almost endless stream of military campaigns. Cities that fell to an invading army one year would be back in Thai control the next. Sometimes the trouble came from the Burmese to the east, at other times from the scattered hill tribes of the north, or from the Cambodians in the west.

Throughout the Ayutthayan period Siam remained the region's dominant power. At its most powerful its borders extended over much of modern-day Laos and Cambodia. Their rulers were forced to pay tribute to Siam.

When the first foreigners, Portuguese who had sailed up from Malacca, arrived in Ayutthaya in 1512 they were accorded a warm welcome. Others followed: Dutch and English traders, French missionaries in the 17th century and a motley assortment of adventurers who found constant work as mercenaries in the king's army. By the 1680s a powerful anti-Western group at court began to resist the growing encroachment of these foreigners or *farang*. The Dutch had forced the king to grant them monopolies over portions of Siam's external trade; the French were earnestly attempting to convert the king to Christianity; and, worst of all, a Greek adventurer, Constantine Paulkon, was made a Thai noble and became one of the sovereign's leading advisers.

Adventurer with strong influence: Constantine Paulkon

In 1688 the opposition acted. When the King died of illness, the foreigners were expelled and for the next 140 years there was minimal contact between Siam and the West. The wars, however, continued. The Burmese by now were the main threat and in 1767, after a long siege, they finally succeeded in capturing and destroying Ayutthaya.

The Founding of Bangkok

Phraya Taksin, a provincial noble, repelled the Burmese invaders. He moved the capital some 40 miles south to Thon Buri, a settlement on the west bank of the Chao Phraya river. There the new king was safe from further attack. The settlement's river location was also of economic value, being well-placed to benefit from trade with Chinese merchants.

When Taksin started to imagine himself as an incarnate Buddha he was overthrown in 1782 in favour of Chakkri, one of his generals. Chakkri decided almost immediately to move the capital yet again. This time the royal porters did not have so far to go. The new royal city was moved across the river to Bangkok (or Krung Thep in the Thai language, meaning the City of Angels). Chakkri, Rama I, was the first king of the Chakkri dynasty that continues to rule the country to this day (King Bhumibol Adulyadej, the present monarch, is Rama IX).

***Chakri, Rama I**, was the first king of the Chakkri dynasty that continues to rule the country to this day (King Bhumibol Adulyadej, the present monarch, is Rama IX).*

In the 19th century Europe was beginning to take a renewed interest in Siam. Traders in particular considered Siam a country rich in natural resources. They came seeking sugar, pepper, cardomans, tortoiseshell, ivory, ebony and rosewood. Some made more unusual discoveries. Briton Robert Hunter came across 'a strange animal swimming in the river: four arms and four legs surmounted by two heads, all moving in perfect co-ordination through the water.' The year was 1824 and the 'strange animal', then aged 13, was named In and

Chan. Two Chinese boys were joined together at the chest: the first Siamese twins.

For the religious, this nation of 'unconverted' souls was too great an opportunity to overlook. Starting in the 1820s all the major Christian denominations sent out missionaries, and the generous Thais allowed them to establish missions in Bangkok. On 23 August 1828 the first Protestant missionaries arrived. They brought with them a printing press to issue religious works, the first ever seen in Siam. The missionaries did much to introduce western ideas. Their attempts to convert the Thais, however, proved largely unsuccessful.

On 18 July 1835, Dr Dan Beach Bradley, an American Baptist missionary, arrived with his family. He used the printing press of the American Missionary Association to publish the very useful *Bangkok Calendar* each year from 1858 until his death in 1873.

In 1839 Siam's first printed government document appeared: a proclamation outlawing opium. Only five years later, in 1844, Bangkok's first newspaper was published.

Along with the missionaries came a steady stream of official representatives, the majority British, seeking to negotiate trading agreements with Siam. Although individual traders were permitted to settle in the country, no agreement was signed formalising their rights. Doing business proved an endlessly frustrating task for these early traders.

***In and Chan**, the original Siamese twins, were discoverd by Mr Hunter, a trader, who became their supporter. In 1829 they left Siam for good. A sensation for both the medical world and the public, they were exhibited as a living spectacle in Europe and America.They became American citizens and even married, producing a total of 22 children between them. They died in 1874 at the age of 63, Chan first, In two hours later.*

An outing to the ruins of the ancient capital ***Ayutthaya*** *at the turn of the century*

Anyone arriving with a cargo of goods had to go through a long and arduous ritual of negotiation with the Thais to establish the official selling price. It was accepted etiquette to bring gifts to offer the king and his officials, and one cynic advised that 'ships trading with Bangkok should bring three cargoes, one of presents for those in high places, one for bribes to the customs officers and one for purposes of trade.'

As the century progressed so the fledging capital developed, containing as it did three distinct communities. Obviously, there were the Thais, symbolised by the walled enclave, the official heart of Bangkok, containing the royal palace. The Chinese settled in Bangkok in huge numbers. They came to dominate the city's mercantile activity. Stores, factories and later hotels were invariably run by them. Finally there were the Europeans. As trade increased they built warehouses and business premises along the river's eastern bank.

This river, the Maenam Chao Phraya (meaning the 'mighty mother of all waters' and in the past usually referred to by foreigners simply as the Menam or Meinam), acted as the capital's main thoroughfare. Its length was dotted with foreign ships which moored there. In place of roads the rest of the city was dissected by canals, or *klongs*, which earned Bangkok a new nickname: Venice of the East.

The rebuffing of the various envoys who had called at the royal palace over the years seeking formalised trading agreements had only put off the growing clamour among Western powers keen to make inroads into Siam. It would take a great leader to steer Siam through the treacherous waters of colonial expansion and gunboat diplomacy. That man was King Mongkut, the fourth member of the Chakkri dynasty. Succeeding to the throne in 1851 he quickly realised that Siam could not resist foreign demands indefinitely. Britain was expanding its possessions in both the Malay Peninsula and Burma; the French had established a firm footing in Cochin China, and even the once mighty Chinese Emperor had been forced to succumb to Western military force, ceding Hong Kong to the British in 1842 after the Opium War.

His Majesty, ***Maha Mongkut****, with a favourite wife.*

When Sir John Bowring, Queen Victoria's governor in Hong Kong, arrived in Bangkok in 1855 he was accorded a warm welcome. The result was the Treaty of Friendship and Commerce with Britain. Siam finally placed trade on a regulated basis. A low scale of tariffs was fixed for imports and exports. Britain was allowed to establish a consulate with extraterritorial powers over British subjects residing in Siam and on 10 June 1856 Mr Hillier, the first British consul, arrived in Bangkok. The other powers were quick to follow in signing similar treaties and by the end of the 1850s the river bank was lined with these new consular offices.

The expatriate community split itself into four distinctive groups. There were the consular officials, the merchants, the seamen and finally the missionaries. As they settled down to life in this far-flung eastern port, so the amenities needed for a comfortable life abroad developed. There were stores, offering everything from sail repair to freshly baked bread; clubs, which no self-respecting expatriate could do without; and, catering to both visitor and resident alike, the city's first modest hostelries.

Now the capital's first roads were built and gas street lighting introduced. To learn more fully from the West, King Mongkut hired a number of foreign advisers and technicians, and, wishing for his children to be educated in English, he sent to Singapore for a governess.

Anna Harriette Leonowens, our friend from the first chapter, duly arrived in Bangkok to fill this post on 15 March 1862.*

**Anna travelled up from Singapore accompanied by her son Louis, her two servants, Moonshee and Miriam Beebe, and her beloved dog, Bessy.*

The 1946 film Anna and the King of Siam, *(directed by John Cromwell, starring Irene Dunn as Anna and Rex Harrison as King Mongkut) and Rodgers and Hammerstein's musical* The King and I, *made into a film in 1956, (directed by Walter Lang, starring Deborah Kerr, Rita Moreno and Yul Brynner) are based loosely on Anna's experiences while in the capital of the Kingdom of Siam.*

The ***'Venice of the East'*** *in 1878. The map shows in detail the location of foreign businesses, houses and missions and indicates the mooring places of overseas shipping. (The Oriental Hotel has been specially highlighted for this publication.)*

(ROUGH SKETCH)
A. J. LOFTUS
TOPOGRAPHER & SURVEYOR
TO H.M. THE KING
1878

CORRECT LOCAL TIME
IS KEPT AT THE
BRITISH CONSULATE

MA NAM CHOW PHYA

STEAMERS LEANING BANGKOK WITH AN EBB
TIDE USUALLY COME UP HERE TO TURN

KLONG BANGKOK NOI

KLONG KUT

AMERICAN MISSION (GIRLSCHOOL)
VANDYKE & FAMILY

WAT RAKANG
GOV. DOCK YARD
LARGE SHEARS
ROYAL FOUNDRY
KING COLLEGE

KING'S PALACE

MI-NISTER OF THE NORTH

INTERSECTED BY
KLONG BANG KA NAK

WAT SAKET
LEADS TO THE LOTUS GARDEN

THE ROYAL PALACE

PALACE OF H. R. H. PRINCE ONG NOI
KING'S GARDEN
TELEGRAPH OFFICE

KLONG MAWN
HIGH TEMPLE.
(WAT CHANG)

INTERNATIONAL COURT
WAT PO

MANY CANALS

POPULATED.

GOV. MEN OF WAR

PALACE OF
H. R. H.
PRINCE ONG YIE
BRADLEY PUBLISHER & PRINTER

POK JIM
PHYS. GASSAR
B.A. NUISE

THE NEW MAIN ROAD
SAM PENG MAR KET
GREAT CHINESE & KLINY BAZAR

KLONG PADOO SEME
MAI

WAT GULLEAH
PRA NAI REEN
SANTA
CHIT PHOTOGRAPHER
CATHOLIC CHURCH
ITALIAN CONSULATE
KING'S SECRETARY

DRAW BRIDGE
KLONG BANG LANG
WAT DOKMAI
CHOW KLANG
PR SUNTERA
REGENT GARDEN

KLING SHOPS
KLING BAZA
POK SHIN SOO
BAR HONG

WAT
REGENT CANAL

H.E. THE PRA NAI
H.E. KALAHOME
HIS THE EX-REGENT

H.E. THE FOREIGN MINISTER'S ZOOLOGICAL GARDENS.
GARDEN PHYS. MUNLOK H.E. THE KALAHOME HOUSES & GARDENS

HOK PO.
POH TEK
GRASSI
ARCHITECT

MOORED

PO SENG

COM. OF POLICE CAP
GERMAN CONSULATE
AUSTRO-HUNGARIAN
CUSTOMS
HARBOR MASTER & PILOTS OFFICE CAP RUSH
DANISH DOCTOR
BRITISH CONSULATE (POST OFFICE)
FRENCH CONSULATE
DANISH CONSULATE
ORIENTAL HOTEL
APOTHECARY (B. GRIM)
DE BAY SOTTE GENERAL STORE

ORCHARDS GARDENS
WATERED BY MANY SMALL CREEKS

POH HEW
PHYA CHA DUT

LEADS TO RATBOORE

(CAUTION!)
WAT
SUNKEN WRECK & LAND SLIP
SEVERAL ARCHORS HAVE BEEN LOSE HERE

THIS IS THE ONLY SUITABLE
PLACE FOR BEACHING VESSELS
IN THE EVENT OF FIRE OR OTHER
CASUALTY AN OLD HULK
GERNERALLY MARKS THIS SPOT

BANGKOK DRYDOCK COMPANY
PREINISES
PROTESTANT CHURCH
BOR-NEO COMPANY
AMERICAN CONSULATE
SWEDISH & NORWEGIAN CONSULATE
PICKENPACK THIES & Co.
R.M. WINDSOR & REIDTICH
R.M. MARKWALD'S
R.M. POH CHINSOO
DUTCH CONSULATE
R.M TAR KIM CHING

NAI SIN
R. M.

TIDAL KLONGS THE
GREATER NUMBER OF THEM
ARE NOT AVAILABLE AT L. WATER

EUROPEAN HOUSES
1 Mr. HAWETSON
2 CAPt RICHLIEU
3 " LOFLUS
4 Mr. ALABASTER
5 " CHANDLER
6 Dr. GOWAN
7 Mr. CLUNIS
8 CAPt WATRONET
9 Mr ROSS & CORDU
10 " DE-SA
11 " DAVIDSON
12 CAPt NICKS

AMERICAN MISSON
R. M.
PICKERPACK
THIES & Co.

SINGLE
SHEAR

SAW MILL D. MAC LEAN & Co.
R. M. B. C LIMITED
TIMBER & SHIP BUILDING YARD.

FISH RAFTS
BONNEVITTE & Co.
TIMBER YARD
BANGKOK SAW MILL

LATITUDES & LONGITUDES

ROYAL PALACE	13° 45′ 28″	100° 27′ 58″
WAT CHANG	" 45 13	" 27 46
H.G Ex. REGENT	" 44 20	" 28 15
H.E. KROMATAH	" 44 36	" 28 28
BRITISH CONSULATE	" 44 00	" 29 27
HARBOR MASTER	" 44 07	" 29 20

.... SINGNIFIES FLOATING HOUSES

M. RICE MILL W. WHARF

S. SMITH'S OFFICE
SIAM WEEKLY ADVERTISER

NOTE. THE NEW MAIN
ROAD IS LINED WITH
TRADES MENS SHOPS-MARKETS
&C. &C. &C.
13 BANGKOK WHARF
14 BAY YUNG SENGS & Co.

YARDS
440 880 1320
1 STATUTE MILE
EACH SMALL DIVISION = 85 YARDS.

NOTE, FOREIGN MEN OF WAR USUALLY MOOR ABREAST OF THEIR RESPECTIVE CONSULATES.

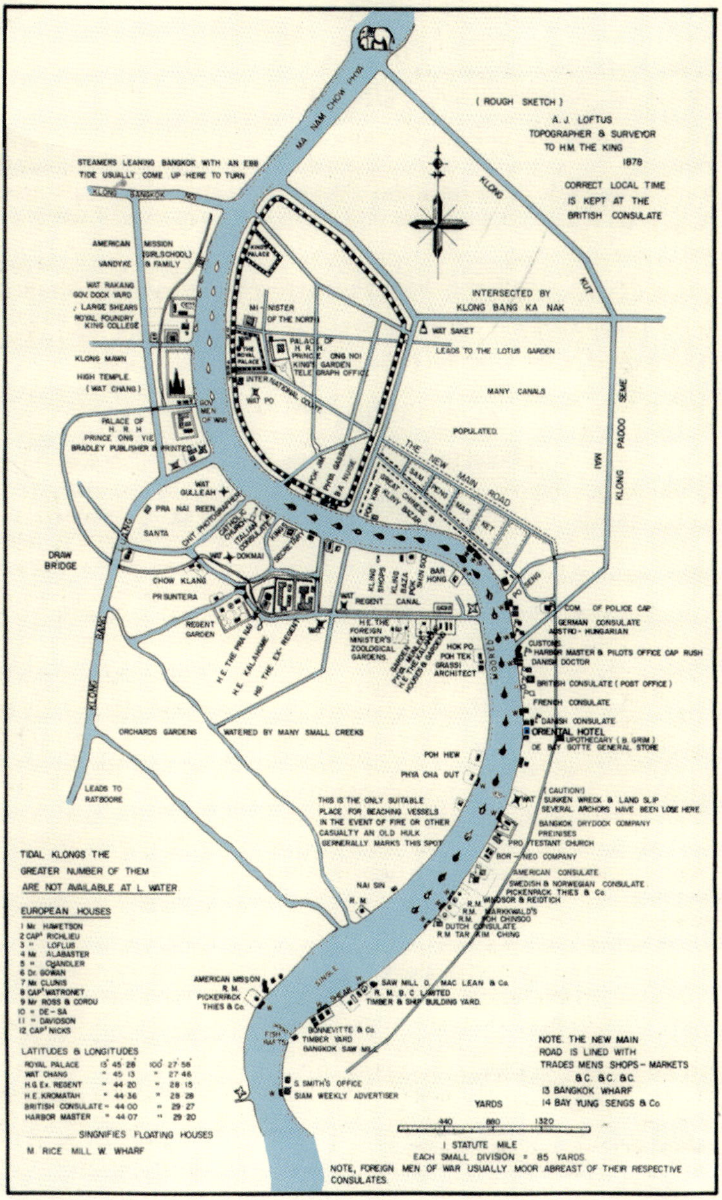

THE EAST ASIATIC COMPANY, LTD.

Head Office: COPENHAGEN

Shipowners, Forest Concessionaires,
Sawmillers, Estate & Mine Owners

Importers & Exporters

OWN OFFICES:

BANGKOK		SINGAPORE	
Bombay	Harbin	Melbourne	San Francisco
Buenos Aires	Hongkong	Mexico City	Sao Paulo
Calcutta	Johannesburg	Montreal	Seattle
Cape Town	Karachi	New York	Shanghai
Dairen	Kuala Lumpur	Penang	Sydney
Durban	London	Port Elizabeth	Tokyo
Hamburg	Madras	Rangoon	Tientsin
Hankow	Manila	Saigon	Tsingtao

Vancouver B.C.

Bangkok Branch: ORIENTAL AVENUE

Cable Address: ASIATIC *Telephone: 31020*

Travelling became fashionable and the ocean liners the grand hotels of the seven seas. The opening of the Suez Canal in 1869 not only gave the world the opera Aida *(Giuseppe Verdi originally wrote this work for the opening ceremony) but faster communication between Europe and Asia. Instead of 32 days the journey now took only nine.*
The East Asiatic Company *advertised its services until the 1960s.*

'How old is this establishment?' is one of the first questions asked about any famous historic hotel.

Modesty is not a consideration when answering: the older the better. These grand old ladies look upon longevity as a blessing and go out of their way to stretch the truth. An architect's first hesitant blueprint is all that is needed to start counting, even if the plan was not translated into bricks and mortar for years afterwards.

The Opening Puzzle

1862 — 1868

he correlation between the development of new means of transport and the evolution of the hotel industry is obvious. The advent of tourism gave the world 'grand' hotels. The term grand hotel was not only a synonym for grandeur. It was a technical expression, too. It was an invention of both innkeepers and architects, the second fulfilling the new requirements of the first. A grand hotel was – and is – a self-contained world which, for the first time, combined all the aspects of hospitality: accommodation, catering, laundry, exchange services, telephone operators, sports and social facilities like clubs or regular meeting places. Hotel garages even catered for local transport *(see list of grand hotels on the following pages)*.

First trade and politics, later leisure and tourism, were the driving forces behind the provision of accommodation for foreigners. Usually it required a type of accommodation both outstanding and glittering compared to the immediate environs, so creating luxury embedded in poverty.

In the second half of the 19th century the grand hotels along the shipping routes of Asia became famous oases of luxury in a desert of poverty. The Galle Face in Colombo, the E&O Hotel in Penang, the Hotel de l'Europe, the Adelphi and the Raffles in Singapore, Hotel des Indes in Jakarta (then Batavia), the Bela Vista in Macao and the

Hong Kong Hotel in the British Crown colony opened their doors.

Thailand, with its cautious approach to diplomatic relations with the rest of the world, developed slower. Bangkok was not an automatic port of call when travelling from, say, Singapore to Hong Kong. When trade relations started to grow and the country opened up to the rest of the world, Bangkok became an increasingly important destination.

It was at this point that The Oriental came into being.

'How old is this establishment?' is one of the first questions asked about any famous historic hotel. Modesty is not a consideration when answering: the older the better. These grand old ladies look upon longevity as a blessing and go out of their way to stretch the truth. An architect's first hesitant blueprint is all that is needed to start counting, even if the plan was not translated into bricks and mortar for years afterwards.

In contrast The Oriental is more reticent about her age. To discover the truth one has to politely accept the age to which she is prepared to admit, while quietly adding to this total. As with any ageing beauty, her good looks and carefully maintained façade can easily deceive.

The exact date of the opening of the hotel is lost in the mists of history. A newspaper entry dated as early as 1863 provides a first possible clue: 'Captain James White, owner of a boarding

Noël Coward

a regular visitor to the grand hotels of the East, at The Oriental:
'There is a terrace overlooking the swift river where we have drinks every evening watching the liver-coloured water swirling by and tiny steam tugs hauling rows of barges up river against the tide. It is a lovely place and I am fonder of it than ever.'

19TH CENTURY HOTELS *of* ASIA & AMERICA

SHEPHEARD'S, CAIRO, 1841
SUISSE, KANDY, 1850
NEW ORIENTAL, GALLE, 1863
GALLE FACE, COLOMBO, 1864
GEZIRA PALACE (Cairo Marriott), CAIRO, 1865
BELA VISTA, MACAO, 1870
GRAND, YOKOHAMA, 1873
HILL CLUB, NUWARA ELIYA, 1876
ORIENTAL, BANGKOK, 1876
ANNAPURNA, KATHMANDU, 1879
EASTERN & ORIENTAL, PENANG, 1885
WINTER PALACE, LUXOR, 1887
WINDSOR, MELBOURNE, 1887
RAFFLES, SINGAPORE, 1887
GRAND, CALCUTTA, 1890
IMPERIAL, TOKYO, 1890
MENA HOUSE, GIZA, 1890
DES INDES (DJALAN GADJAH MADA), JAKARTA, 1897
MAIDEN'S, DELHI, 1898
MOUNT NELSON, CAPE TOWN, 1899
CATARACT, ASWAN, 1899
GRAND DE PEKING, BEIJING, 1900

WILLARD, WASHINGTON D C, 1850
MILLS HOUSE, CHARLESTON, 1853
PARKER HOUSE, BOSTON, 1855
MENGER, SAN ANTONIO, 1859
BALSAMS GRAND, DIXVILLE NOTCH, 1866
MOHONK MOUNTAIN, NEW PALTZ, 1869
PALMER HOUSE, CHICAGO, 1870
ROYAL HAWAIIAN, HAWAII, 1872
PALACE, SAN FRANCISCO, 1875
SAGAMORE, BOLTON LANDING, 1883
CHELSEA, NEW YORK, 1884
STRATER, DURANGO, 1887
JEKYLL ISLAND CLUB, JEKYLL ISLAND, 1887
DEL CORONADO, SAN DIEGO, 1888
JEROME, ASPEN, 1889
CHATEAU LAKE LOUISE, ALBERTA (CAN), 1890
PLAZA, NEW YORK, 1890
BROWN PALACE, DENVER, 1892
HISTORIC VANCE, STATESVILLE NORTH, 1892
CHATEAU FRONTENAC, QUEBEC, 1893
PFISTER, MILWAUKEE, 1893
WALDORF–ASTORIA, NEW YORK, 1893
JEFFERSON, RICHMOND, 1895
GREAT SOUTHERN, COLUMBUS, 1897

19TH CENTURY HOTELS *of* EUROPE

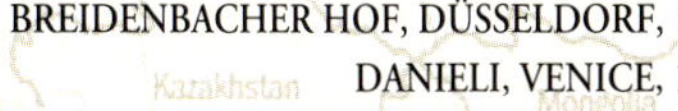

BREIDENBACHER HOF, DÜSSELDORF, 1813
DANIELI, VENICE, 1822
SHELBOURNE, DUBLIN, 1824
NASSAUER HOF, WIESBADEN, 1830
DES BERGUES,GENEVA, 1834
BROWN'S, LONDON, 1837
SAVOY BAUR EN VILLE, ZURICH, 1838
BAUR AU LAC, ZURICH, 1844
VALTIONHOTELLI, PUNKAHARJU, 1845
WESTMINSTER, PARIS, 1846
INGHILTERRA, ROMA, 1850
SEILER HOTEL MONTE ROSA, ZERMATT, 1853
VIER JAHRESZEITEN, MUNICH, 1858
GAUER HOTEL SCHWEIZERHOF, BERNE, 1859
BEAU-RIVAGE PALACE, LAUSANNE, 1861
DE PARIS, MONTE CARLO, 1864
DE L'EUROPE, HEIDELBERG, 1865
LANGHAM, LONDON, 1865
VICTORIA JUNGFRAU, INTERLAKEN,1865
ÖSTERREICHISCHER HOF, SALZBURG, 1866
AMSTEL, AMSTERDAM, 1866
ATHÉNÉE (PLAZA ATHÉNÉE), PARIS, 1867
GRAND HOTEL, VIENNA, 1870
CAP EDEN ROC, ANTIBES, 1870
BRENNER'S PARK, BADEN-BADEN, 1872
PALACE, TURIN, 1872
GRAND HOTEL DUCH D'AOSTA, TRIESTE, 1873
BÜRGENSTOCK, 1873
IMPERIAL, VIENNA, 1873
GRAND HOTEL, OSLO, 1874
GRANDE BRETAGNE, ATHENS, 1874
GRAND HOTEL, DAVOS, 1875
GRAND HOTEL EUROPE, ST. PETERSBURG, 1875
LE RICHEMOND, GENEVA, 1875

GRAND HOTEL ET DES PALMES, PALERMO, 1875
SACHER, VIENNA, 1876
FRANKFURTER HOF, FRANKFURT, 1876
INTER CONTINENTAL, PARIS, 1878
MONT BLANC, MEGÈVE, 1880
DES INDES, THE HAGUE, 1881
GRAND HOTEL VESUVIO, NAPLES, 1882
KRASNAPOLSKY, AMSTERDAM, 1883
HASSLER, ROME, 1885
SPLENDIDE ROYAL, LUGANO, 1887
PANHANS, SEMMERING, 1888
FÜRSTENHOF, LEIPZIG, 1889
SAVOY, LONDON, 1889
REID'S, FUNCHAL, 1891
BRISTOL, VIENNA, 1892
PERA PALAS, ISTANBUL, 1892
DU PALAIS, BIARITZ, 1893
GRAND, ROME, 1894
MÉTROPOLE, BRUSSELS, 1895
DE L'EUROPE, AMSTERDAM, 1896
GRAND HOTEL PUPP, KARLOVY VARY, 1896
PALACE, ST MORITZ, 1896
VIER JAHRESZEITEN, HAMBURG, 1897
CONNAUGHT, LONDON, 1897
BAYERISCHER HOF, MUNICH, 1897
BRITANNIA, TRONDHEIM, 1897
CLARIDGE'S, LONDON, 1898
RITZ, PARIS, 1898
MÉTROPOLE, MOSCOW, 1898
DOLDER GRAND, ZURICH, 1899
GREAT CENTRAL, LONDON, 1899
CONTINENTAL, OSLO, 1900
VILLA IGIEA GRAND HOTEL, PALERMO, 1900
EUROPA, PRAGUE, 1901

The 'bread basket' of the kingdom was the delta of the ***Menam river****. It flooded annually between June and November, the waters attaining their greatest heights in August. The floodwaters covered several thousands square miles and provided ideal conditions for growing rice, a crop which furnished two-thirds of Siam's total exports. During the floods vast quantities of fish swam into the rice-fields and were left behind when the water receded, thus providing another valuable and abundant food supply.*

In 1884, for example, 419 vessels and 143 junks arrived in Bangkok with cargoes valued at £27,170. 240 of these, with a total tonnage of 151,984, were British. The total value of exports reached £2,262,240 in 1884, rice being the principal earner.

Imports were valued at £1,044,255, the chief

house for seafarers at the river Menam, drowns while crossing the river.' Unfortunately the name of the boarding house is not mentioned. Was it The Oriental? It might well be as there was no other boarding house along the river at that time. A man called Gustav Falck had opened the eponymous Falck's Hotel in 1863, but Falck's wasn't *at,* but only *near,* the river.

Two years later, another catastrophe pitches The Oriental into the headlines by name for the first time. On 11 June 1865 a fire started in the riverside premises of a trading firm called Virgin & Company. The official report in the annual *Bangkok Calendar* stated:

'Another 69 buildings were destroyed in the ensuing conflagration including the Oriental Hotel. The hotel is located on the east side of the river on land belonging to the Privy Purse, a little below the French consulate.'

Further historical facts concerning the early days of the hotel are scarce and fail to solve the question of when it first opened.

The official answer was given over one century later. During the 1970s the board of the hotel decided to end the uncertainty. They agreed that it would be questionable, not to say inauspicious, to use the burning of The Oriental in 1865 as the founding date.

1976 heralded the opening of the new River Wing and so, putting history to work, the hotel was declared a hundred years old. Giorgio Berlingieri, director of the hotel and co-founder of Italthai, the major stockholder in The Oriental, explained his decision:

'It is poetic license. And we are not exaggerating. We are a hundred years old when we could give an even more impressive figure.'

Everybody therefore is happy with the hotel's official date of birth: 1876. And historians can rest assured: they will be able to find proof that the hotel existed even earlier.

Our story continues in 1864 with the completion of the New Road. It was Bangkok's first modern thoroughfare and ran along the river bank linking the palace with the foreign consulates. On 26 October 1866 gas street lighting was introduced to the capital. These gas lamps threw a bright light on events surrounding the development of the boarding house at the Menam river which would grow into one of the most famous hotels in the world.

The city was totally different from today's Bangkok: only one decent road, no hotels, no restaurants or bars. There was no hospitality industry for there were no foreigners to make use of it. In short, no tourism. Travellers

items being grey and white shirting.

Despite being outlawed 704 chests of opium were also imported. The surplus revenue earned from exports was paid in Mexican silver dollars, which were melted down and recoined. This silver coinage also became Siam's standard of weight. The currency system, however, was based on a confusing system as follows:

The fuang = 7 $^1/_2$ cents, the salung = 15 cents, the baht or tikal = 60 cents or half a crown; 5 tikals = 3 Mexican dollars.

From the tikal upwards the coins were also used as measures of weight. Thus 1 tikal weighed 15 grammes or 231 grains; 4 tikal = 1 tamlung, 20 tamlungs = 1 chang or catty; two Chinese catties = 3.2lb. There were also gold coins, but not in general circulation. Their value was 16 times their weight in silver. Here's to the metric system!

General Ulysses S Grant *arrived in Bangkok as part of a round-the-world trip. An account of his trip was written by John Russell Young who was especially impressed by the city's major means of transport. 'You are told that Bangkok is the Venice of the East, which means that it is a city of canals. When the tides are high you go in all directions in boats. Your Broadway is a canal. You go shopping in a boat.'*

Grant's term as 18th President of the United States of America had finished in 1877. He stayed as a guest of King Chulalongkorn at the Suranrom Palace. Today a US State visitor would occupy the entire River Wing of the Oriental Hotel. Grant, who travelled with his wife and their son Jesse, had already met Pope Leo XIII and Her Majesty, Queen Victoria, in Europe. During his five-day visit to Siam he had an audience with the king and attended a State dinner held in his honour.

were a rare sight. A handful of seamen came to the city but invariably slept on board their vessels. Missionaries arrived and proceeded to their missions. Diplomats were accommodated at their consulates or in private residences.

The Oriental Hotel developed accordingly. When Bangkok was merely a port of call for trading ships on their way from Hong Kong to Singapore The Oriental was a seamen's home; a boarding house where one could sleep, eat and drink; a place where one found shelter from torrential monsoon rainfall. Later, of course, when the means of transport became more luxurious, The Oriental reflected this change.

In 1868 Rama V, King Chulalongkorn, was crowned king. He continued the reforming ways of his father and Bangkok grew into a trading port of increasing international importance. Anna Leonowens, King Mongkut's governess, had left Bangkok one year earlier, again on board the *Chao Phya*. She was never to return to Siam.

King Chulalongkorn with his sons

Bombyx mori

Saturnia Cecropia (South American Silk Moth)

Saturnia Pernyi (Chinese Silk Moth)

Saturnia Cynthia

Silk Moths – busy workers in the Thai export industry in the 1870s

Although silk has been known from antiquity, it was produced exclusively by the Lao communities settled throughout the country, the chief centres being Korat and Battampong. The total export of silk in the late 1870s was around 300 cwt per annum, valued at approximately £20,000.

In the Course of a Day

Every day the terrace undergoes various metamorphosis: from breakfast venue with a rich and healthy buffet to a sunset meeting point where the first sun-downers are absorbed in style and finally the dinner terrace with a lavish barbecue buffet. And occasionally it seats 1.700 guests watching José Carreras life in concert.

S Cardu created the most elegant public dining-room in Bangkok

THE FIRST STEPS

1870

–

1893

HM

Andersen

Conrad

hen the city's trade grew The Oriental's unique situation on the river helped make it the principal rest-house in the capital of Siam. C Salje, a Danish seaman, bought the hotel in the 1870s and moved it one big step closer to what may be considered a civilised home away from home. In 1878 he placed an advert in the annual *Siam Directory*: 'Family accommodations.—American Bar, Billiard Saloon, Baths, Newspapers kept, Boats for hire, Table d'Hôte, Breakfast 9 A. M., Tiffin 1 P. M., Dinner 7 P. M.'

A fellow Dane, H Jarck, managed the hotel. In 1880 the two Danes started bottling mineral water. In 1881 they retired and returned to Denmark. Hans Niels Andersen, who had formed Messrs Andersen & Co, became the new proprietor of the Oriental Hotel, the nearby Oriental store and ship chandlery, the Oriental ice factory, the Oriental bakery, an aerated water manufactory and the Koh-Si-Chang Hotel and store.

In 1885, the year Upper Burma was annexed by Britain, Andersen decided to rebuild the Oriental Hotel in a style befitting its growing popularity with the capital's merchants and seamen. He commissioned a local Italian architect, S Cardu, to design the new building. S Cardu had established his offices in Bangkok in 1880. The Italian designer created a structure that, having withstood over a century of change, still stands at the heart of the hotel and is now known as the Authors' Wing.

The Oriental was the first luxury hotel in Siam. Never had such richness been seen in Bangkok outside the palace: carpets covered the hallways, there was artistic wallpaper with the latest designs from Paris and the bedrooms on the second floor were furnished with mahogany rattan. A second floor! What a sensation for a country of floating houses and one-storey bungalows.

The newly established *Bangkok Times* was less than five months old when it announced the hotel's 'Grand Opening Day' scheduled for Thursday, 19 May 1887: 'The new hotel will open to the public for the first time. A banquet for 180 honoured guests will be held on the hotel's lawn to the accompaniment of two orchestras.'

When the big day arrived hundreds of curious sightseers roamed the gardens, the new hall, the iron staircases and the terrace. Young Siamese in crowded boats on the river could hardly believe their eyes when watching men and women swaying in one another's arms to the sound of music.

Professor Maxwell Sommerville, who was to arrive at The Oriental a decade later, wrote: 'When a European colonist had the courage to build this, the first great hotel, all classes of Siamese opened wide their eyes with wonder.

Hans Niels Andersen: *born on 10 September 1852 in the small fishing village of Nakskov in Denmark, he had left the poverty of his early years to pursue a career at sea. He had arrived in Bangkok via Hong Kong in 1873. Having made money and a name for himself by taking a cargo of teak to England against the monsoon and returning intact with a profitable hold full of coal, he formed Messrs Andersen & Co with his partners, Peter Andersen and Frederick Kinch.*

Somebody was fashioning an ark in their midst. As they gazed on its enormous proportions, many said, with mouths charged with betel-nut, "Tam chi, tam chi" ("Please yourself, please yourself"). The inference was that, should the travellers arrive, they would never be willing to climb all those steps and be lodged up in the air, as until then they knew only one-story habitations. So for months other voluntary Siamese inspectors, throwing their heads and their hands in the air, cried, "Tam chi, tam chi." The enterprising host took that advice, and in pleasing himself has pleased all those who wish to see the "City of the Invincible, Beautiful, Royal Archangel!" This is the significant name of the city of Bangkok.'

George Troisoeufs was installed as manager of the hotel. The first major function he supervised was a banquet in honour of Queen Victoria's Golden Jubilee. Troisoeufs decorated the new building from top to bottom. Throughout the dinner several bands played splendidly and it was past ten o'clock before the dancing began. Fireworks brightened the sky before midnight, concluding with a royal salute of 101 guns. A congratulatory telegram was sent to Her Majesty informing the Empress that a Jubilee Victoria Ward at the local hospital had been established in her honour. Prince Svasti, the Lord Mayor of Bangkok, remained until after midnight, highly gratified with the hospitality he received. The Oriental was at her most beautiful and delighted guests stayed until four o'clock in the morning when the musicians struck up *Rule Britannia*.

The dinner was such a success that expatriates and Siamese society declared The Oriental *the* place for important parties. The food and service were superb, the drinks chilled and on top of all this a unique location by the river – what more could one ask for?

From now on journalists and travellers did not stop talking about The Oriental. Rarely was a letter sent from the Venice of the East without mentioning that elegant and comfortable hotel. 'There is only one hotel, the "Oriental", now existing in Bangkok,' wrote Norwegian Carl Bock on his visit in 1884.

In 1887 the hotel opened its own bakery. The same year horse-drawn trams were introduced along New Road. The oldest guest records date back to January 1888. A Mr N Lazarus, an optician from Calcutta, offered free eye examinations while staying in room 5. His name in the guest book was followed by a certain Mr Knight (a decorator specialising in the re-covering of billiard tables), J Iwi (a precious stones dealer) and R Lambert (a carriage dealer).

One man did not register at the hotel that year although he was a frequent visitor to the bar of the hotel. On 24 January 1888 Józef Teodor Konrad Korzeniowski, born in

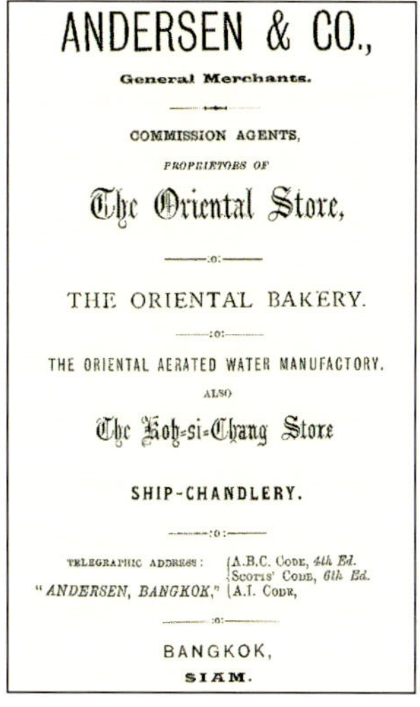

1881

Messrs Andersen & Co became the new owners of the Oriental Hotel, the nearby Oriental store and ship chandlery, the Oriental ice factory, the Oriental bakery, an aerated water manufactory and the Koh-Si-Chang Hotel and store.

Joseph Conrad in 1888
While in Bangkok, overseeing the reloading of the ship and waiting for the crew to recover from illness, he spent many evenings swapping stories in the bar of The Oriental. 'We talked of wrecks, of short rations and of heroism . . . and now and then falling silent all together, we gazed at the sights of the river.'

December 1857 in Poland and better known as Joseph Conrad, arrived in Bangkok to take over command of a ship, the *Otago*. The previous captain had died at sea.

Early in the morning of 8 February 1888 the *Otago* weighed anchor and glided quietly past the foreign consulates and the still-slumbering occupants of The Oriental on her way to Singapore. This was to be Conrad's only visit to Bangkok and in fact his first and only sea-going command. A few years later he traded the helm for a pen and, settling in England, took up writing full time. Conrad's experiences with the *Otago* provided material for a number of his stories including *Lord Jim*, *The Shadow Line*, *Falk* and *The Secret Sharer*. Here fact and fiction merge so that it is almost impossible to tell the two apart. But Bangkok continued to have a strong hold on his mind and he utilised every moment of his experience in the east in his writing, embellishing here, enhancing there, until even the old timers at the Oriental bar would have been proud of him.

On 22 September 1888 The Oriental made another step towards being officially accepted by the palace. A dinner was given at the hotel by HRH Prince Prisdang, Director General of the Post and Telegraph, for the officials in his department.

This year also marked an important juncture in the commercial development of the capital.

The first branch of the Hong Kong and Shanghai Bank in Bangkok opened for business, a sign of the city's growing economic importance.

The *Bangkok Times* reported in March 1889: 'The Oriental proprietors are showing their determination to make the whole place attractive in a novel way, at least for Bangkok. Two admirably constructed fountains adorn the grass plots in front of the Hotel, and at night act considerably in cooling the atmosphere and refreshing the star-gazers in the neighbourhood for nothing.'

HM King Chulalongkorn *paid a private visit to the hotel on 17 December 1890.*

In 1890 the guest list slowly grew more cosmopolitan and on one day it included patrons from Hamburg, New York, Rome, Cardiff, Singapore, Bombay, Delhi, and Geneva. In January a dinner was hosted by Mr C Donner, the Singapore Belgian Consul, for his counterparts in Bangkok. The highlight of the year happened on 17 December. Mr Allen, the new manager, together with Mr Andersen welcomed the most prominent guest the hotel had ever seen: His Majesty, King Chulalongkorn. The king arrived with his entourage to assess the ability of the hotel to host guests of the palace. His Majesty was truly impressed and so decided to accommodate the Crown Prince Nicholas of Russia, who became Tsar in 1894, at The Oriental in April 1891.

During a visit ***Lt G J Younghusband*** *noted: 'A visit to Bangkok at once proclaims to the traveller the preponderance of British influence. Half the European residents are English; shopmen have their signboards painted in English; English is the language of the Telegraph Department; and the Siamese postage stamps and coinage have English inscriptions. The public buildings have their names engraved in English above the portals. In fact, to the casual observer, Bangkok appears as much English as Aden. From a British point of view these proclivities are most encouraging.'*

◊◊ —— ◊◊

***The* Bangkok Times**, *founded in January 1887, an invaluable source of tales about the hotel.*

31 January: *on this very Wednesday evening, a copy of Bacon's* Essays *changed pockets rather daringly.*

Shortly before the Russian prince's arrival the *Bangkok Times* announced: 'A new European manager for the Oriental Hotel has lately arrived from Hong Kong in the person of Mr Smith, the former proprietor of the Astor House in Shanghai. Mr Smith has had 37 years' experience of hotel life and his valuable service ought to prove advantageous to the Oriental Hotel.' Smith was followed by George F Kornloff who, 'as manager of the well-known local rendez-vous, the Oriental Hotel, is maintaining the reputation he gained at the Adelphi in Singapore as a first-class caterer and courteous host.'

An advert for The Oriental in the *Directory for Bangkok and Siam* of 1891 modestly declared: 'Largest and best appointed hotel in Siam. . . . Magnificent view of the Meinam. . .. A steam launch conveys passengers and their baggage to and from all Mail Steamers. . . The splendid new Bar, together with the Billiard Saloon, Reading and Smoking Rooms, Ladies Room, &c., is fitted with every convenience. The Bedrooms are lofty, well ventilated, and open on to large verandas, with bathrooms.'

The 'splendid' bar was indeed well stocked. The wine list was impressive. French and German wines, from Mouton Rothschild to Liebfrauenmilch, dominated the supply. Beers ranged from Pilsen to Flensburg, with Spaten, Marstrand, Carlsberg and stout beer.

The principal drawing-room reflected the cosy atmosphere of the house. Armchairs, sofas, an ottoman, flower stands and vases, Brussels carpets, crystal chandeliers over the piano and two large 'looking glasses' helped create an intimate atmosphere. Even more personal was the private pink drawing-room. Here photographs of the Thai king and queen graced the wall.

The epitome of elegance was the private blue drawing-room with a bedroom (No 1) en suite. Today it would be the presidential suite. The inventory list from this period includes sofas, armchairs, a conference table with six chairs, a table clock, flower stands, paintings, a crystal chandelier, blue silk curtains with holders and mosquito curtains over the beds.

The bar was teakwood with a marble top. Next to it stood two large billiard tables, surrounded by five sofas. A portrait of George Washington overlooked the room. The card-room next door offered five card tables and three chess boards.

In the principal dining-room were four tables with 48 chairs and four punkahs. Punkahs were a common sight all over Asia. They came originally from India. Natural ventilation and stenghas (whisky with soda) or pink gins (gin with a drop of Angostura bitter) were not sufficient to keep guests cool and so rooms were furnished with punkahs, sheets of canvas,

Whether it was returned by the gentleman thief as requested by its indignant owner, we will never know.

27 April:

an engineer named F A Hitchcock was thrown out of the hotel after misbehaving and also for not paying his bills. Nevertheless he returned and made for the bar. Mr Andersen tried to intercept him. Hitchcock drew back, pulled a revolver from his coat and tried to shoot Andersen. Perhaps he had already visited a bar elsewhere for he missed, the bullet striking the wall of the billiard room instead. Hitchcock was placed in the British consular jail awaiting trial.

1 June:

The proprietors of The Oriental gave the use of the hotel's hall to a group of male residents (including Messrs Halliday, Heck, Arnold and Cook) wishing to practise for a series of musical evenings.

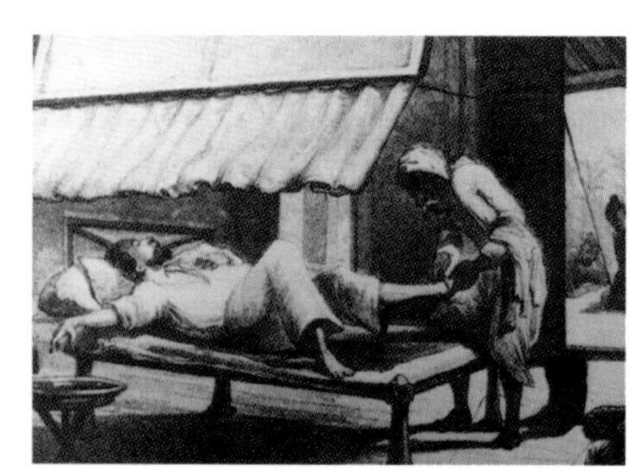

Punkah wallahs:
to keep guests cool, rooms were furnished with punkahs, sheets of canvas, hanging from the ceiling, pulled to and fro by means of a cord, creating a delightful breeze.

hanging from the ceilings. These precursors of air-conditioning were pulled to and fro by means of a cord, creating a delightful breeze. In many cases the cords were tied around the big toe of punkah wallahs, boys of Indian origin, who were posted outside the rooms. They moved the sheets of cloth continuously and legend has it that the punkah wallahs were even able to keep operating the fans in their sleep.

There were two more private dining-rooms on the ground floor. Bedrooms No 1 (the 'Presidential Suite') to No 19 were located on the upper veranda.

In September 1890 Bangkok's first electric light generating system was inaugurated. The hotel had electric light from April 1891 onwards.

The railway age had arrived in the Kingdom of the White Elephant.

One of the most interesting features of the illumination of the 19, 20 and 21 September 1891 in honour of the king's birthday was a 'grand ornamental exhibition of electric light at the Siam Electric Light Co.'s works, the royal palace and the Oriental Hotel.' Soon the city's tram system was electrified and in 1893 King Chulalongkorn personally opened Siam's first railway, a 16-mile length of track running from the capital to Paknam near the mouth of the Chao Phraya. The railway age had arrived in the Kingdom of the White Elephant.

Supported by the king, a full programme of railway building ensued. The first major line was to run to Korat in the east (chosen to improve accessibility to an area where the

— ¤ —

'The first important objects seen, in approaching the city, are the Bangkok dock premises on the west, the Oriental Hotel, and the French consulate'

– ¤ –

Directory for Bangkok and Siam, 1891

French were threatening the kingdom's eastern border). This line opened in 1900. That same year work began on a line to the south which by 1903 had reached Petchaburi. Finally, in 1909, Siam signed an agreement with the Federated Malay States allowing the line to be extended to the Malayan border where it linked up with the Malayan Railways.

In 1893 difficulties between France and Siam reached their climax. Siam had acted as a buffer between British and French interests. Now French colonialist Eugene Etienne proclaimed in *La Cocarde*: 'Siam will inevitably be taken over by us or by them one day; better that the morsel falls to us.' French colonialists, encouraged by French annexations in Africa and the Pacific, wanted to acquire the whole of Siam. In expanding Indochina they wanted to rival British India. The very existence of the Siamese kingdom was at stake. Three French warships anchored on the Menam river in September 1893, directly in front of the Oriental Hotel. Thankfully the crisis was ended without bloodshed. The price for Siam was the payment of a war indemnity of three million French francs and the cession of certain territory, including a portion of the State of Luang P'rabang, to the French. A longer-term solution came several years later.*

The Kingdom of Siam remained independent, its survival ensured by the Great Power rivalry between Britain and France.

* *'The Anglo-French Declaration of London in 1896 was crucial to the survival of Siam,' writes Patrick Tuck. 'It placed crippling restrictions upon the ability of the French colonialists to threaten the independence of the kingdom. For this reason it also devolved upon the Siamese far greater control over their own predicament.'*

Anchoring in front of the French Legation: the Lutin, *the* Inconstant *and the* Comète.

The roof and upper storey of the Oriental Hotel can be seen in the background.

BANGKOK, July 1th. 189[illegible]

Bar = Stock. June 30th. 1892. Dr.

To the ORIENTAL HOTEL.

ANDERSEN & CO., Proprietors.

Qty	Unit	Item	Price	Amount
			✓	160.12
2	qrts.	Medoc.	3.—	3.—
8	pts.	Medoc	1.80	1.20
5	qrts.	St. Julien	4.80	2.40
9	pts.	St. Julien	3.—	2.25
6	qrts.	Pauillac	70	11.20
10	qrts.	Leoville	80	5.60
7	qrts.	Pontet Canet.	90	6.30
8	pts.	Pontet Canet.	50	9.—
5	qrts.	Mouton Rothschild	1.35	6.75
2	pts.	Burgundy.	1.—	2.—
8	qrts.	Pommard	1.25	10.—
7	qrts.	Beaune	80	5.60
3	qrts.	[illegible]	8.10	2.70
0	qrts.	Hochheimer	12.—	10.—
4	qrts.	Geisenheimer	12.—	4.—
3	qrts.	Geisenheimer Rothenberg	12.—	8.—
3	qrts.	Liebfrauenmilch	15.—	3.75
5	qrts.	Johannisberger	15.60	7.80
5	qrts.	Heidsiecks White seal	2.10	10.50
4	pts.	Heidsiecks white seal	110	4.40
5	qrts.	Heidsiecks monopole.	270	13.50
		4 dry monopole. qrts.	290	11.60
9	pts.	Heidsiecks Monopole.	145	4.35
2	qrts.	Mumm & Co. extra dry.	3.—	6.—
11	pts.	Mumm. & Co. extra dry	165	18.15
11	qrts.	Krug & Co.	2.—	22.—
3	qrts.	Cyder.	4.50	16.11
5	pts.	Cyder.	3.—	1.50
7	qrts.	Barsac	9.—	5.25
1	qrts.	Sauternes.	13.80	2.30
1	qrts.	Ch. Yquem.	24.—	4.—
3	qrts.	Larose	22.—	5.50
1	qrts.	Margaux	11.40	1.90
[illegible]				

Received Payment.

BANGKOK, July 1th. 1892

Bar-Stock June 30th. 1892

To the ORIENTAL HOTEL,

ANDERSEN & CO., Proprietors.

3	qts. Sherry	90	2 70
6	qts. Port Wine	90	5 40
4	qts. Vermouth French	65	2 60
3	qts. Vermouth Ital.	65	1 95
4	qts. Brandy xxxx	165	6 60
3	qts. Brandy xxx	165	4 95
2	qts. Sherry brandy Kirschbaer	1.20	2 40
4	qts. Kirschbaer	80	3 20
2	qts. Tafel aquavit	65	1 30
2	qts. Kummer aquavit	70	1 40
2	qts. Hosters Magenbitter	1.–	2 –
4	pts. Angostura Bitter	95	3 80
1	pts. Orange Bitter	[illegible]	[illegible]
2	qts. Rhum Jamaique	90	1 80
2	qts. Carlshamn Punch	90	1 80
1	qts. Genever		– 90
1	qts. old Tom		– 70
1	qts. French bitters		– 90
5	qts. Pilsener bier	2.90	1 45
10	qts. Flensburger bier	2.90	14 50
70	pts. Flensburger beer	1.90	7 43
40	qts. Spaten beer	3.–	10 –
16	qts. Marstrand beer	2.90	11 15
2	pts. Marstrand beer	1.90	3 47
5	qts. Carlsberg beer	2.90	8 46
4	pts. Carlsberg beer	1.85	11 42
7	pts. Bass beer	2.–	2 83
5	pts. Stout beer	1.80	6 75
9	qts. Flottbeker export beer	2.90	7 02
3	qts. Munke Brau	2.90	18 39
9	qts. Liqueurs diverse	2.25	20 25
			160.12

Received Payment,

1892

Stocklists of the hotel's bar always reflected that simple maxim of 'only the best'. Medoc, Mouton Rothchild, Heidsieck Monopole, Liebfrauenmilch . . .

This Indenture made the fifth day of June 1893 Between Hans Niels Andersen, Peter Andersen and Frederick Kinch all of Bangkok (hereinafter called the vendors) of the one part, and Franklin Hurst also of Bangkok (hereinafter called the purchaser) of the other part.

Whereas the said vendors have for some years past carried on the business of the Oriental Hotel in the messuage and premises situated at Bangkok and comprised in a certain deed of lease dated the 1st of January 1888.

And Whereas the said vendors are also entitled to certain steam launches carriages, furniture, utensils, stock-in-trade chattels and fixtures used in the said business, which are fully specified in the Schedule hereto attached.

And Whereas the said vendors have agreed with the purchaser for the sale to him of the goodwill of the said business, together with the steam launches, carriages, furniture utensils, stock-in-trade, chattels

Contract of Sale

From Hans Niels Andersen Peter Andersen and Frederick Kinch

To Franklin Hurst

Dated the 5th June 1893

The contract of sale between Hurst and the former owner, Hans Niels Andersen, is one of the rare documents about the early years of the hotel to have survived. We owe this to the methodical methods of the East Asiatic Company in Copenhagen rather than to any local depository where documents are frequently destroyed by ants or other acts of nature.

Goodbye *Mr* Andersen

The Maxwell Sommerville Memoirs

1893 – 1910

Turn your Kodak on the dining-room three times a day . . ., Maxwell Sommerville

The Large Kodak and its smaller brother, the Kodak

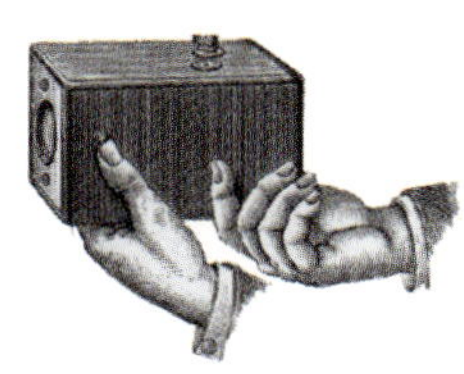

ne more round!' Franklin 'Bill' Hurst* motioned to the bartender. The Chinese cashier scribbled some figures on a 'chit' and handed it to the waiter. They knew the man in the white suit well. Hurst and his friend Louis Thomas Leonowens spent almost every night at the bar. Leonowens was the most famous permanent resident of The Oriental. He was in the teakwood business up in the north. He had buried his wife here in Bangkok in the Protestant cemetery a couple of months ago. Then he had taken his children back to England to stay with his mother, Anna, the former governess of the king of Siam. Since his return he had become a regular patron of The Oriental.

The bartender took the bottle of Dutch gin and poured it over an egg yolk at the bottom of the glass, added a splash of Angostura and completed the concoction with some sugar and nutmeg. He served the Andersen's Special – named after the proprietor himself – to the two men. Louis smiled:

'I remember when I arrived in Bangkok with my mother. The Oriental Hotel was the first thing I saw.'

'When was that?' Bill asked.

'1862, Bill. Thirty-one years ago.' Louis answered. 'I was always fascinated by this building. Of course it wasn't the Oriental Hotel we have today. It was a small house for

Franklin 'Bill' Hurst had come to Siam in 1888 as a member of Sir Andrew Clarke's Railway Survey. After that job he had gone on to manage his own race course society before turning hotelier.

seafarers. But it was there. I remember that I was so disappointed when we had to sleep on board the *Chao Phya* that first night. I would have preferred to sleep here.'

The four men observed a family entering the dining-room. They took a table near the arches that led to the veranda.

'They are doing good business here: 40 bedrooms, a restaurant and the bar,' Bill said to Louis.

'The bar mainly depends on our daily consumption of Andersen's Specials,' Louis added smiling.

'Why don't we buy this place? I have heard rumours that Andersen wants to move out of this sort of business.'

'When the price is right,' Louis nodded.

The price was right. Andersen was happy to sell. He returned to Denmark in 1897 to found the East Asiatic Company along with a certain I Glückstadt, the founder of the Landmans-Banken. Today it is the largest company in Denmark with worldwide interests.

The contract was signed on 5 June 1893. The vendors, Hans Niels and Peter Andersen and Frederick Knich, sold the hotel with its steam launches, carriages, furniture, utensils, chattels, fixtures and stock-in-house for the sum of US$22,000.* *(see next page)

Hurst hired American W J Palmer to manage the property. He had all the furniture repainted

Louis Thomas Leonowens

In 1881 Leonowens returned to Siam. The king employed him as Grand Master of the Horse with the rank of captain and granted him an anual salary of £800. In August 1884 Louis married Caroline Knox and was appointed the upcountry agent for the Borneo Company. Teakwood had become one of Siam's major exports and foreign companies were competing vigorously for the licences to work the northern forests.

Louis T. Leonowens
(LIMITED)
BANGKOK, SIAM
(Head Office: 11-12 Fenchurch St., London, E. C.)

Teak Concessionaires,
SAW MILLERS,
GENERAL
IMPORTERS
AND
EXPORTERS

Large and well seasoned stocks of Teak always on hand. Exporters of Teak Logs, Planks, Boards, Floorings and Scantlings, and all varieties of Sawn Teak material in ordinary trade dimensions, or sawn to special sizes.

SPECIALTIES:
Deck Planking, etc., for Ship-builders.

Scantling for Railway Carriage and Wagon Constructors.

Telegrams, "LEONOWENS BANGKOK"
"DENNY, BANGKOK" (Sawmill)

The Leonowens enterprises

* *US$3,000 were payable in cash upon signature of the contract; US$6,000 by a promissory note payable twelve months after the first day of June 1893. A further US$6,500 was to be received with interest on the first day of July 1895. The balance of US$6,500 was to be handed over on the first day of July 1896.*

and turned the dining-room into one of the prettiest in the Far East. He valiantly launched a campaign to abolish that much abused system of payment known as the 'chit method'.

In 1894 the Chartered Bank of India, Australia & China (incorporated 1853) became the second bank in Bangkok when it opened a branch on a site between the French consulate and the hotel. The bank was rebuilt in 1908 and the passage that separated it from The Oriental became known as Chartered Bank Lane. The land on which the bank was situated would one day become the home of an extravagant new wing for the hotel, but at the time nobody could have foreseen this.

Among the travellers who came to visit during that last decade of the 19th century was Professor Maxwell Sommerville of the University of Pennsylvania. He arrived in 1897, during manager Palmer's time, and the Oriental launch went out to meet him. His detailed account of his stay appears in the margins of pages 64–67. His visit led him to conclude: 'To leave Siam in a parenthesis, to fail to see and to study that interesting people and their country, is like visiting Italy, as many do, without seeing Bologna.'

In 1885 The Oriental was host to HRH Prince Luigi Amedeo, nephew of the King of Italy. He was welcomed as the first royal occupant of The Oriental's best suite. Various festivities continued to take place at 'the only place in

Advertisement in the Directory for Bangkok and Siam, *1894*

Professor Maxwell Sommerville,
professor of glyptology at the University of Pennsylvania, travelling with his wife, arrived at The Oriental in 1897.

'We were impressed with the courtesy of the Siamese from the moment we stepped on shore, which was on a beautiful terrace, shaded by a grove of luxuriant trees, through which sanded paths led to the Oriental Hotel. The manager, an Englishman, proceeded to give us some ideas of the arrangement of the house. The first entrance was into a one-storey garden portal, with six arches built of stuccoed brick, the interior with floor of sand, furnished with hot-weather armchairs and round tables, plentifully supplied with English journals of Bangkok and from the Straits Settlements.

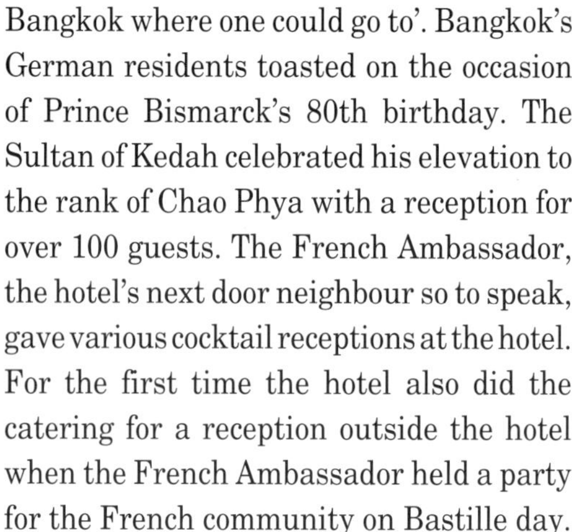

Bangkok where one could go to'. Bangkok's German residents toasted on the occasion of Prince Bismarck's 80th birthday. The Sultan of Kedah celebrated his elevation to the rank of Chao Phya with a reception for over 100 guests. The French Ambassador, the hotel's next door neighbour so to speak, gave various cocktail receptions at the hotel. For the first time the hotel also did the catering for a reception outside the hotel when the French Ambassador held a party for the French community on Bastille day.

In 1899 the eccentric Hurst sold his interests in The Oriental to a syndicate represented by a Mr W Downie. By the turn of the century The Oriental had firmly established itself with Bangkok society and was still a much sought after watering hole for travellers who had no contact with civilisation for a long time. In those days there was no air-conditioned airport building with limousines waiting to provide transport through the city. Journeys were exhausting. Those who did not arrive by ship had to travel overland. In 1901 we find a report of a visit to The Oriental by Edmund Chandler.

'It was dark when the launch deposited Shafraz and myself on the Oriental Hotel landing-stage, and I was so irredeemably disreputable that I had some misgivings as to my reception. But I was permitted to taste the joys of civilisations, and unless one has spent days in a malarious Siamese jungle amongst imbecile savages, without visible means of transport, one cannot duly appreciate the delights of a soft bed, a European *menu*, and the contact with one's own fellow-creatures.'

During the following three years the hotel underwent further improvements and expansion, doubling its capacity and increasing the quality of its accommodation. In 1903 F S Robertson took over the hotel. His period of ownership could hardly have been shorter. Only a few months later he had to leave town in a hurry because of his debts.

In August 1904 The Oriental was forced to close down temporarily while Mr Robertson was charged and tried, thus ensuring that The Oriental's name appeared every day in the *Bangkok Times*.

'Properties pertaining to the estate of Mr R were sold at the premises lately known as The Oriental Hotel', followed by, 'The Oriental is to let unfurnished with or without the annexed houses on the ground floor of the new wing.'

Mr Robertson was never heard of again.

In 1905 a future president of the Siam Society and one of the country's most famous scholars, the late Phya Anuman Rajadhon,

'We passed into the principal hall, about seventy feet broad by thirty feet deep, serving at the same time as reception-room, library, office, general thoroughfare, billiard-room, and buffet, known in many countries as a bar. It is attended by several Siamese, under supervision of two moonshees. These moonshees can work so rapidly and with such precision by the aid of their wire and ball calculator, the abacus, that every English bank throughout the East is compelled to employ them.

'Once you have chosen your room, you are simply known by its number. We were known as Number One. It was the last apartment at the manager's disposal. It consisted of three pieces: a double-bedded sleeping room, a parlour, and beyond that a commodious veranda, well defended from the sunlight by large split bamboo screens. There were two sheets on our bed, which was a luxury we often were denied in India and Burma. Besides the welcome sheets there was a peace-maker…

continued from previous page

A long, narrow bolster covered with white linen and filled with horse-hair: it is placed on the centre of the mattress, from head to foot, and is an important feature on a double bed on a Bangkok night.

'The mosquitoes were so vigorous that at any moment of the night, by quickly closing the hands over the forehead, on an average, eight or ten of these musical creatures would remain helpless on the palms of the hands. We thought it not prudent to speak of these executions to the Siamese room-boys, as they, being Buddhists, would not only lose respect for us, but would regard us as guilty sinners.

'The furniture in our veranda room was all of rattan and cane – deep reclining-chairs and lounges with tables attached. No matter how much we would try to barricade the flimsy, short jalousies at the points of ingress and egress to our apartment, one or other of our native servant boys would find

came to work as a clerk at The Oriental. It was his first job and he was paid a monthly salary of 60 baht. In his memoirs (*Fuen Kwam Lang – Remembrance of Things Past*), Phya Anuman remarked that one could live comfortably on this sum provided one did not indulge in the triple vice of drinking, gambling and womanising. Was he referring to Mr Robertson?!

After the Robertson fiasco The Oriental was nursed back to health by Mr Carl G Edwards, an American from New York before flourishing again under the management of Mme M O Bujault. She engaged a Viennese orchestra, revived the tradition of musical dinners and employed a new chef, Monsieur Brier, straight from France. Mme M O Bujault returned to Europe in 1910.

On 23 October 1910 Siam's greatest and much-loved monarch, HM King Chulalongkorn, Rama V, the father of modern Siam, died. The Oriental flew the black flag. For the next 22 years it was owned and managed by Mme Maria Maire. The following year's coronation of Prince Vajiravudh as Rama VI brought splendid business to the hotel. During the festivities all 40 rooms of The Oriental were fully booked. The city welcomed Prince William of Sweden, Prince Waldemar of Denmark, Grand Duke Boris of Russia, to name but a few. Many foreign journalists choose to stay at The Oriental, including Signor Salvatore Besso who wrote to his wife in Milan: 'We reached Bangkok amid rain, thunder and lightning. The landing at the garden of the Oriental Hotel in that darkness reminded me of the Royal Garden at Venice.'

Rooms No 3 and 4 were engaged by Fabergé, the well-known *bijoutier*. All Bangkok converged there to view the lavish exhibition of his *objets d'art* in the finest Russian enamels and Siberian precious stones. The visit paid off as the new king became a valued customer. The exquisite pieces produced on his instructions included an image of Buddha that is now kept in the temple of the Emerald Buddha.

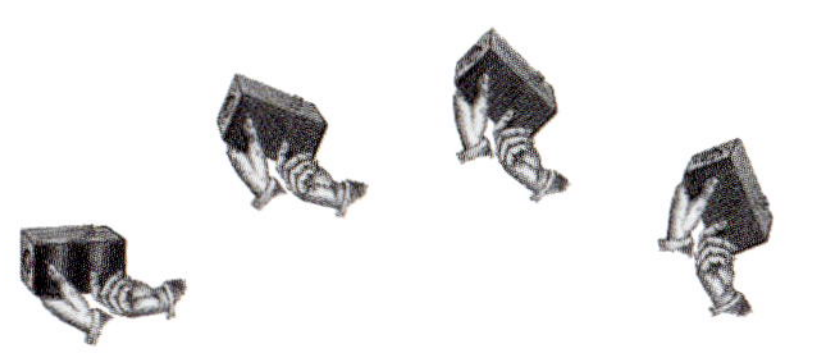

his way into our presence. He felt he must begin our day by serving the inevitable chota hazri, – the early bite, – a cup of tea, toast, and two plantains. These people are so accustomed to see thousands around them without any costume that they have not the slightest curiosity to see how travellers are made up; nor are they indiscreet.

'In almost all other matters this Siamese hotel is not very unlike what one generally finds in the East. Turn your Kodak on the dining-room three times a day, and you will see an efficient corps of Mongolian servants, who in the morning at breakfast, or at noon at tiffin, or in the evening at dinner, are serving mangosteens, bread-fruit, oranges, custard-apples, the health-giving papaya, pineapples, mangoes, and bananas. In the hottest of the hot times of the year, when the griffins are not there, the durian is cut out of doors, and after its unpleasant odour has in a measure passed off, it is served on the table; then it is delicious.'

THE HOTEL IN THE 1920S

Years of economic hardship had left their marks on the surface of the grand old lady. But still it was at The Oriental where travellers got a piece of French soap for their first shower after an exhausting journey up the river on the mail steamer, on the express train from Butterworth or through the jungles of Siam.

Savon
Mylissia
EXTRA FIN

ORIENTAL HOTEL

Bangkok, 20th April 1911

TIFFIN

Celery Soup.
Fried Fish, Red Sauce.
Fried Veal, Caper.
Stewed Chicken.
Cold Beef Salad.
Potatoes.
Siamese Curry.
Baked Custard.
Cheese.
Fruit.
Coffee.

Siam was one of the first countries in Asia to recognise the benefits offered by a new form of travel: aviation.

The Great War

Vaslav Nijinsky dances at the hotel

The Oriental Hotel Company

1911 – 1922

iam was one of the first countries in Asia to recognise the benefits offered by a new form of travel: aviation. In 1911 King Rama VI sent three Engineer Corps officers to France to study aeronautics and they returned in 1913 as fully qualified pilots. That same year aeroplanes were used in military manoeuvres for the first time, but it was the commercial benefits air travel offered, in ending Siam's relative isolation and enhancing communications with the outside world, that caught the attention of the management at the Oriental Hotel. *

In Asia during World War I friends suddenly became enemies. Being British one did not socialise any more with a German subject. An Austrian diplomat was no longer invited to a French garden party.

The news of the war did not initially effect life at The Oriental. The hotel hosted Bangkok's first performance of Molière's play *Le Medecin Malgré Lui*. The occasion was the inauguration of the Alliance Francaise. Then, in 1916, Maria Maire presented Vaslav Nijinsky. Kiev-born Nijinsky, maybe the greatest dancer of the 20th century, gave the first display of classic western ballet in Bangkok.

On 22 July 1917 Siam's declaration of war against Germany burst upon smiling, optimistic Bangkok like a thunderclap out of the blue. Now dinners and concerts at The Oriental

**In March 1924 Imperial Airways was founded. There were four aerodromes in Siam open for international and national flights, situated at Song Khla, Ubon, Chieng Mai and Don Muang, the latter about 13 miles north of Bangkok.*

were held in aid of ambulance funds, the Red Cross and other charities.

Just after the war neither the hotel nor the world of exotic travel were prospering. While local social activities flourished – a monthly dance held at the Oriental Hotel was frequently attended by members of the Thai royal family – The Oriental was affected by the global economic crises.

The Hanoi journal *L'Eveil Economique de l'Indochin*e sent its correspondent, a certain M Henri Cucherousse, to Bangkok in 1920. The journalist took a dim view of the hotel. In an article he called it 'a small place with forty bad, comfortless rooms in an old building on the bank of the river.' While admitting that it had 'two characteristics of a first-class hotel: an entrance hall and a fine dining-room', he deplored its lack of 'a drawing room for ladies' and of 'proper bathing accommodations', and, worst of all, its generally run-down appearance, his impression being that it must be ten years since the place had a coat of paint.'

Henri Cucherousset had dared to attack a national institution. A lengthy, indignant and dignified answer appeared in the *Bangkok Times*. For M Cucherousset's edification and for the benefit of future travellers it contained an account of the hotel's history, including the grand reopening in 1887, a detailed description of the present establishment – 'one of the best in the East' – and a terse rejoinder at the end:

IMPERIAL
GERMAN MAIL STEAMERS,
NORDDEUTSCHER LLOYD, BREMEN.

The Steamers of this Company, subsidized by H. I. G. M's Government, convey Passengers and Cargo every 4 weeks to and from the following ports, viz:—

Bremen, Antwerp, Southampton, Genoa, Brindisi, Port Said, Suez, Aden, Colombo, Singapore, Bangkok, Hongkong, Shanghai, Yokohama, and Nagasaki.

The Above Company has also fast Mail boats plying between Bremerhaven and New York, and, further, a regular Mail Service between the former port and South America.

Particulars regarding dates of sailing, rates of passage money, freight, etc., may be obtained on application at the Company's Agents' office.

BEHN, MEYER & Co.
Agents Norddeutscher Lloyd,
SINGAPORE.

A. MARKWALD & Co.,
BANGKOK,
Sub-Agents.

Mail Steamer to Europe every four weeks

'We think M Cucherousset owes us an apology for his harsh remarks.'

Nevertheless, the past decade *had* left its mark on the world and the hotel in Bangkok was no exception. A fresh coat of paint was long overdue; the water pipes leaked; the driveway needed resurfacing; the roof had not been repaired for years. The problem was raising the money necessary for such renovations. How could a hotel maintain the high standards set in better times?

In 1924 Maria Maire came up with the answer. She founded The Oriental Hotel Company. The new firm raised capital of 60,000 baht, a huge sum for the 1920s. Maire became one of the shareholders and was appointed managing director. Now she was ready to embark upon important renovations.

A year later the necessary work had been completed. A 1927 guidebook stated: the Oriental Hotel is 'the oldest hotel in Bangkok and has long since established and still maintains a reputation as a firm favourite with visitors. It can boast electric light throughout, sample rooms for commercial travellers and a bathroom attached to every bedroom. Tariff (per person per day): single 14 ticals; double 13 ticals; breakfast 2 ticals; lunch 2.50 ticals; dinner 3 ticals.'

While the railways helped fuel Bangkok's growing popularity as a destination for

Telegrams:
ORIENHOTEL, BANGKOK

Oriental Hotel

Bangkok

Oldest and most Popular Hotel in all of Siam. Situated on river front, fine gardens, French Chef. Cuisine and all appointments first class—rates moderate. Our Steam Launch meets all Steamers, also Auto Car at disposal of guests. *Now being remodeled. Modern Toilet Fittings, Etc.* ALL LANGUAGES SPOKEN

Proprietor: A. Maire

In 1924 Maria Maire founded The Oriental Hotel Company, became one of the shareholders and was appointed managing director.

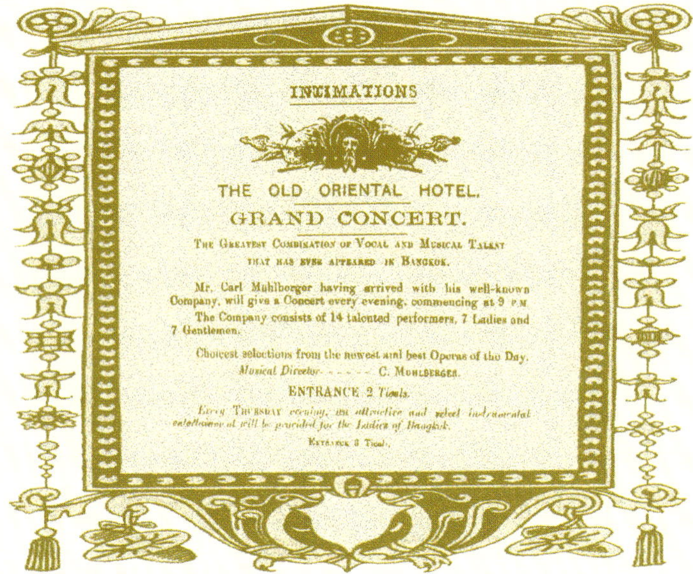

INTIMATIONS

THE OLD ORIENTAL HOTEL.

GRAND CONCERT.

THE GREATEST COMBINATION OF VOCAL AND MUSICAL TALENT THAT HAS EVER APPEARED IN BANGKOK.

Mr. Carl Muhlberger having arrived with his well-known Company, will give a Concert every evening, commencing at 9 P.M.

The Company consists of 14 talented performers, 7 Ladies and 7 Gentlemen.

Choicest selections from the newest and best Operas of the Day.

Musical Director - - - - - C. MUHLBERGER.

ENTRANCE 2 *Ticals.*

Every THURSDAY *evening, an attractive and select instrumental entertainment will be provided for the Ladies of Bangkok.*

ENTRANCE 3 Ticals.

The concert hall at The Oriental was the centre of Western arts in Bangkok. The start of World War I did not initially effect The Oriental. Just before the war the hotel's concert hall had been successfully transformed into a theatre.

travellers in the interwar years, they also ushered in the first serious challenge to the Oriental Hotel's previously unquestioned position as the city's leading hotel. Plush new hotels such as the Hotel Trocadero, the Hotel Royal, where the chef had previously worked at Claridges, opened and began to compete with The Oriental for business. Most guests remained unmoved by these changes. Realising that The Oriental offered far more than just first-class accommodation, they stayed put and Maire continued to welcome travellers from all over the world. People carried the name Oriental Hotel all over the globe.

TROCADERO HOTEL

THE PREMIER OF HOTEL DE LUXE OF SIAM

(and according to the "Record"—journal issued by the Ministry of Agriculture and Commerce).

One of the Most Up-To-Date Hotels in The Far East.

Under experienced European Management.

Opened in September, 1929.

View of Building of the Trocadero Hotel

Situated in The Centre of The Business Quarter.

Large cool airy bed rooms and sitting verandahs all are handsomely furnished, having its own private bathrooms with hot and cold running water.

LIFTS TO ALL FLOORS.

Cuisine renowned through SIAM and neighbouring countries being under the supervision of a well known Parisian Chef.

Best Service.

BEAUTIFUL DINING SALOON.

MAGNIFICIENT SPACIOUS LOUNGE.

Guides can be supplied for tourist.

L. GAY, MANAGING DIRECTOR.

The twenties brought the first serious challenge to the Oriental Hotel's previously unquestioned position as the city's leading hotel. Plush new hotels such as the ***Hotel Trocadero*** *opened and began to compete with The Oriental for business. The published rates at the Trocadero were 12–15 ticals for a single with bath, including meals (compared with 14 ticals at The Oriental). Dinner for non-residents was available in both hotels priced 3 ticals.*

To the left is a 1920s portrait of a well-dressed Siamese mother and her teenage children. They belong to the family that owned the Trocadero Hotel.

The grand entrance hall: Isn't that waltz by Johann Strauss?

Somerset Maugham Suite

1923 – 1945

Somerset Maugham was to Asian hotels what Imelda Marcos is to shoe shops today. It is no secret that some hotel boys learnt his name from room doors rather than from books.

Maugham

A New Pace

World War II

omerset Maugham was to Asian hotels what Imelda Marcos is to shoe shops today. When he arrived in Bangkok in 1923, he had already visited practically every hotel of note in the Malay Peninsula. Many have since honoured his visit by naming their own Somerset Maugham Suite. It is no secret that some hotel boys learnt his name from room doors rather than from books.

The day Maugham set foot on the lawn of the Oriental Hotel is still well remembered, if not to say sacred. The author travelled in the company of his friend Mr Haxton. He arrived by train from Chiang Mai. It was 6 January 1923. 'I was in Bangkok. It is impossible to consider these populous modern cities of the East without a certain malaise. They are all alike, with their straight streets, their arcades, their tramways, their dust, their blinding sun, their teeming Chinese, their dense traffic, their ceaseless din. They have no history and no traditions. Painters have not painted them. No poets, transfiguring dead bricks and mortar with their divine nostalgia, have given them a tremulous melancholy not their own. . . . But when you leave them it is with a feeling that you have missed something and you cannot help thinking that they have some secret that they have kept from you.

'The hotel faced the river. My room was dark, one of a long line, with a veranda on each side of it, the breeze blew through, but it was stifling. The dining-room was large and dim, and for coolness' sake the windows were shuttered. One was waited on by silent Chinese boys. I did not know why, the insipid Eastern food sickened me. The heat of Bangkok was overwhelming. The *wats* oppressed me by their garish magnificence, making my headache.'

Somerset Maugham arrived by train from Chiang Mai. It was 6 January 1923.

Maugham felt ill: 'I took my temperature. I was startled to see that it was a hundred and five. I could not believe it, so I took it again; it was still a hundred and five.'

Maugham had contracted malaria while travelling. 'Towards the end of my journey down Siam the officer in command of the post had insisted that I should stay in his own house. He gave me his best bedroom. I had not the heart to say that I preferred my own little camp-bed, which had a mosquito-net, to his, which had not. The anopheles snatched at the golden opportunity.'

Maugham fell seriously ill at the hotel. It was a bad attack. For some days the quinine had no effect on him. One morning he overheard a conversation between Mme Maria Maire, and the doctor. 'I can't have him die here, you know. You must take him to the hospital.'

The doctor replied: 'All right. But we'll wait a day or two yet.'

'Well, don't leave it too long,' she replied.

Only a few days later Maugham suddenly recovered. 'And because I had nothing to do except look at the river and enjoy the weakness that held me blissfully to my chair I invented a fairy-story.' *

In 1925 Maugham was back in Bangkok, stopping again at The Oriental, and he stayed for two weeks in perfect health, much to Mme Maire's relief. On his last visit to Bangkok in 1960 to celebrate his 85th birthday he reminisced: 'I was almost evicted from The Oriental because the manager did not want me to ruin her business by dying in one of her rooms.'

* *This story can be found in the book* The Gentleman in the Parlour.

William Somerset Maugham *(1874–1965). British writer of Irish origin, born in Paris. Read philosophy and literature at Heidelberg and qualified as a surgeon at St Thomas's Hospital, London.*

Books:
Liza of Lambeth *(1897)*
Of Human Bondage *(1915)*
The Moon and Sixpence *(1919)*
Short stories like Rain *were published in* The Trembling of a Leaf *in 1921*
Cakes and Ale *(1930)*
The Razor's Edge *(1945)*
Quartet *(1945)*
Plays:
Lady Frederick *(1907)*
East of Suez *(1922)*
Our Betters *(1923)*

'Travel from London to Bangkok in only nine Days!' the Aerial Transport Co of Siam proudly announced in 1930.

The pace of life underwent a curious change. People suddenly started to rush round the world rather than travel leisurely. The world braced itself for the age of mass transportation. Large passenger liners were launched and aircraft were constructed to carry more and more patrons.

Bangkok Noi station was built in the suburb of Thonburi on the river's west bank. On 1 January 1927, King Prajadhipok opened the first bridge to span the Menam. This carried the railway across the river, thus linking the southern and northern systems at the central station of Hua Lampong. In April 1932 the king inaugurated the Menam River Bridge which finally established a means for pedestrians and vehicles to cross between the left and right banks.

Before long Bangkok's streets were choked with all manner of wheeled vehicles, but it was the arrival of the motor car at the turn of the century that led to the traffic nightmare, that is now a fact of life for anyone visiting Bangkok.

The new Ford Tudor was a fashionable sight on the streets of the city. The car was available at £185.

Walter B Harris, commander of the Ouissan Alaouite of Morocco, visited Bangkok in 1928. The tyranny of the motor vehicle was in full swing.

'Pedestrians and jinrickshas were scattered right and left in a pandemonium of noise, for not only is the Siamese chauffeur a scorcher of the deepest dye, but he delights also in an exaggerated attention to his klaxon and hooter. He spends all his spare cash in adding to his car as many of these inhuman instruments as he can collect. He drives well, it must be allowed, from the trick-driving point of view. He escapes ninety-nine accidents by a hair's breadth for every one he indulges in. But the one he does meet with is generally final. Driving in a taxi in Paris is like a gentle promenade in a bath-chair compared to an outing in Bangkok.'

The Oriental Hotel responded to the growing supremacy of road traffic, and the growing number of guests who now arrived by car, by moving its main entrance to the side of the building, which could be reached from Oriental Avenue.

'Travel from London to Bangkok in only nine Days!' the Aerial Transport Co of Siam proudly announced in 1930. 'America now only fifteen days distant, Japan six days, Hong Kong two

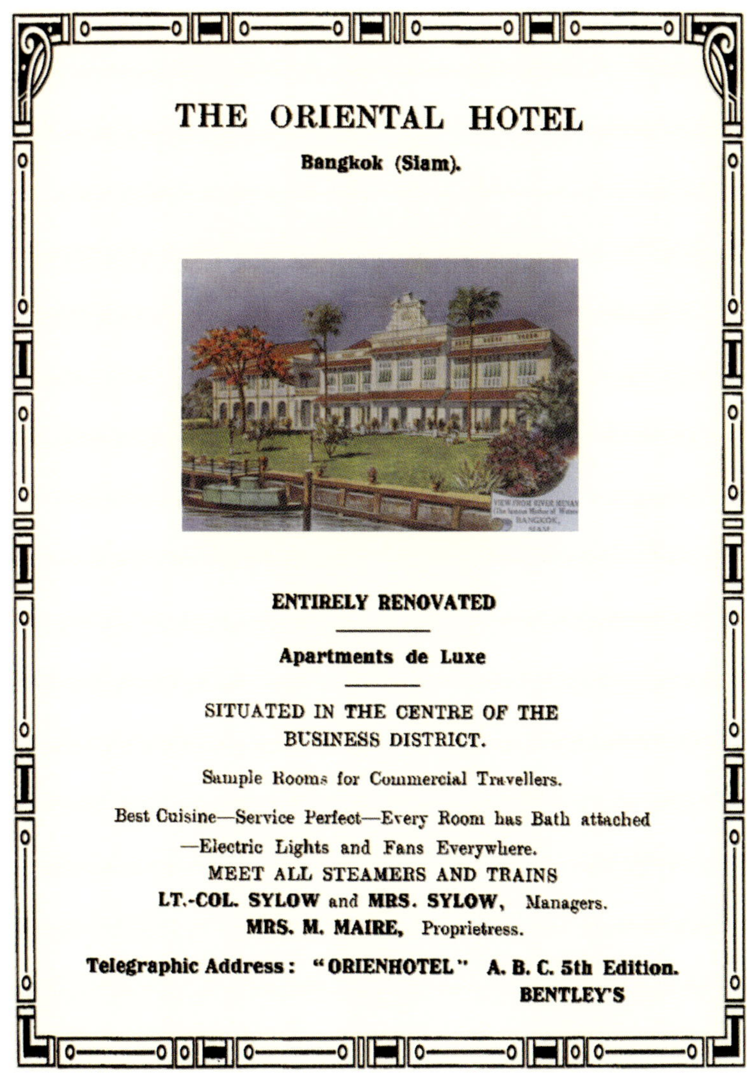

An advertisement that appeared in 1932 in the Guide to Bangkok *by Major Eric Seidenfaden. 'This hotel is situated on the river front . . . It is the oldest hotel in Bangkok . . . lighted all through with electric light . . . every room has bath attached.*

Douglas Fairbanks arrived in style on the liner Belgenland *in 1931 and took residence at The Oriental.*

days.' The flights across the Pacific to the States were more a series of hops than a long-haul journey: Hong Kong, Tokyo, Guam, Wake, Honolulu . . .

The first group of aerial travellers landed at Don Muang airport in 1931, among them Mr and Mrs C H Day, The Oriental's first airborne guests. When Douglas Fairbanks came to stay at The Oriental he preferred classic means of transport. He arrived in style on the liner *Belgenland* in 1931.

W Robert Foran, a guest of the Oriental Hotel during the 1930s, made an interesting comment about the growing Japanese presence not only in Siam but all over the Malayan Peninsular:

'The great majority of the professional photographers throughout Malaya, Siam and the neighbouring territories are Japanese. They are to be found in almost every township – watchful, polite, and yet inscrutable. Personally, I am inclined to believe that every Japanese traveller is a potential secret service agent; or, at least, is collecting and forwarding information likely to be helpful to his own country . . . which should prove of inestimable value should the day unhappily arrive when East and West are in conflict.'

This conflict was still years away. The most significant change occurred on 24 June 1932. Discontented elements among the country's educated ruling class, calling themselves the People's Party, staged a bloodless coup which finally brought to an end Siam's days as an absolute monarchy. King Prajadhipok signed the nation's first constitution in December that same year and a national assembly was duly convened.

In March 1932 Maria Maire departed after 22 years at the hotel to get married in London.

'When Mme Maire took over,' ran one of the newspaper articles dedicated to her, 'the only method for ordinary folk to reach Bangkok was by water. There were no trains to Chiang Mai or restaurant cars to Prae, not to mention this new means of airborne transport and life was a good deal pleasanter than now.'

One modern feature the Sylows had not yet installed was a swimming pool and in April 1933, on a particularly scorching day, ***Barbara Hutton*** *had to go to the Sports Club for a dip after sightseeing.*

Lt Col and Mrs Sylow took over from Maria Maire and set about adapting The Oriental to the newly arising needs of Siam's capital city. One modern feature the Sylows had not yet installed was a swimming pool and in April 1933, on a particularly scorching day, Barbara Hutton had to go to the Sports Club for a dip after sightseeing.

W Robert Foran, who took advantage of the railway network of the peninsula on his visit to Bangkok in 1933, noted that, 'since the completion of the southern section of the Siamese State Railways, and its connection with the railway system in British Malaya, travel into this fascinating little kingdom has become quite a simple matter. From Singapore to Bangkok by rail is only 1,200 miles, and can be covered in fifty-two to fifty-three hours.' Today the luxurious Eastern and Oriental Express has revived this romantic service on the old route.

'As acting on the advice given me in Penang, I had already telegraphed for accommodation at The Oriental. The hotel porter met me on arrival at Bangkok Noi station. He brought a message from the proprieties, suggesting that I might find it more pleasant to detrain here and travel down river to the hotel in a motor-launch. That was a most thoughtful act. In about thirty minutes we came fussily to a halt at the private landing-stage of the Oriental Hotel.

'The hotel is within a stone's throw of the British Legation; and every business place of importance is close at hand, as well as the principal clubs. Electric light and fans, modern sanitation and comfortable rooms were not the least of the attractions of this hostelry. The cuisine was at least as good as that of the best hotels in the East or Far East; and I enjoyed a fillet steak there, which was as tender and sweet as any served in the great capitals of Europe.'

In 1935, the year of Ananda Mahidol's succession as king, The Oriental proprietors and managers, the Sylows, left Bangkok and Mr J O Hossig tried in his turn to enhance The Oriental's prestige. In order to regain the old sparkle he staged a sumptuous dinner for two hundred, offering many special treats for his guests by hiring the best orchestra in town, buying all the latest gramophone records and commissioning a Siamese artist to paint a panoramic frieze of Alpine scenery round the dining-room.

After that he decided to vary the menu. In addition to the hotel's already famous French cuisine, *Smorrebrod* now became one of The Oriental's specialities. Another Hossig special was his Christmas programme, the merriest in town.

In 1936 Charles H Holmes and his wife, who set off on the 12,754-mile journey from Brisbane to London, set a whirlwind pace unimaginable to their predecessors. One typical day's itinerary read as follows: 'Breakfast–Batavia; lunch on plane; dinner–Singapore.'

On the fifth day of their journey, the couple reached Don Muang aerodrome in Bangkok where 'brown men took and sealed our camera lest we should photograph the rice fields or the canals or the *wats* and *bots*, the last two being the terms in Siam for monasteries and temples respectively.'

The Holmes, as the vanguard of a new breed of globetrotter, inevitably took rooms at The Oriental: 'Our room at the hotel was allotted by a Frenchman and a native boy entered with the largest "Flit" gun I've ever seen, and set out disconcerting the mosquitoes which apparently

The old Post Office

'The hotel is within a stone's throw of the British Legation; and every business place of importance is close at hand, as well as the principal clubs.' (W Robert Foran)

take a siesta beneath the bed during the day, for there the boy concentrated most of his attention. My wife went to open the window, but retreated with an exclamation as two lizards darted up the glass to the ceiling.'

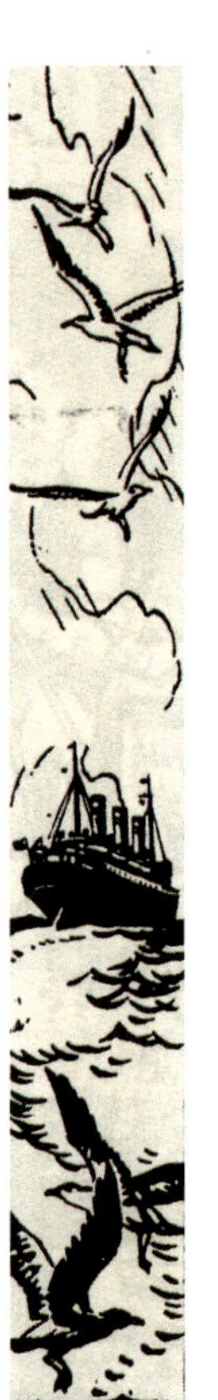

Another feature of the hotel that remained unchanged was the convivial company to be found in the hotel's lounges, where stories were exchanged and views expounded just as they had been in Joseph Conrad's day. On their first evening the Holmes fell into conversation with two Englishmen and from them learnt that the nation's traditional affinity for things English had waned. Holmes discovered that 'Siam is said to be developing a marked preference for Japan, and Japan a marked interest in Siam, where she holds big business interests. If Japan's aspirations extend to Siam, wedged between British Burma and French Indo-China, that country will assume vital importance and will be a pivot on which great events may hinge in Far Eastern affairs.' Prophetic words indeed.

An era was drawing to a close and, as if to signal this change, on New Year's Eve 1937, H N Andersen died in his native Copenhagen, an international figure, at the age of 85. Andersen, the man who had started life in such poverty, was hailed in death as 'the most outstanding personality in Danish commercial life'. He could be proud of his achievements: the founding of the East Asiatic Company

1 January 1927, King Prajadhipok opened the first bridge to span the Menam.

which, *The Times* reported in its obituary, became 'one of the few Danish firms to gain a name known all over the world'; the establishment of a fleet of ships that was 'seen in all the harbours of the world'; his tireless diplomatic efforts during World War I when 'he undertook the perilous journey across the North Sea 16 times to negotiate with the British Foreign Minister, and he had several talks with King George V; he became the only Dane outside the royal family to be presented with the Order of the Elephant, Siam's highest honour; but his most enduring legacy was a simple, two-storey structure, surrounded by gardens, on the bank of Bangkok's Menam River: the Oriental Hotel.

So much had changed since those far-off days and to drive home the point *The Times* also carried short obituaries for E R Sheepshanks, Bradish Johnson and Edward Neil, three young journalists covering the civil war in Spain, who were killed when their car received a direct hit from a shell.

Before long, however, the Siamese government had fallen under the control of the military, and the rest of the decade was to be characterised by increasing nationalism at home and a growing friendship with Japan. In 1939, as part of this policy, Siam's name was officially changed to Thailand, meaning *free country*; heavier taxation was introduced, affecting the Chinese and many European firms in particular; Chinese immigration was curtailed; and inroads were made into the foreign domination of the nation's mining, lumber and shipping industries.

War clouds were gathering around the world and the following year, as German tanks rolled across the plains of Europe, Japanese troops began a blockade of French Indochina. In December 1940, sensing that Thai interests would best be served by a closer relationship with the Empire of the Rising Sun, the two governments signed a treaty of friendship. It was to pay only short-lived dividends. In March the next year Thailand, as a result of Japan's ultimatum to the Vichy government in France, was ceded Laos and part of Cambodia, territory which had been handed over to France under different circumstances fifty years before.

Thailand officially declared its intention to remain neutral in the event of war in south-east Asia, but when on 8 December 1941, as *Zero* fighters pounded American ships at Pearl Harbour, Japanese troops crossed the Thai border, the government soon acquiesced in this *fait accompli*. After initially offering Imperial forces permission to cross Thai territory, the government later went the whole way and in January 1941 formally declared war on Britain and the United States. An important footnote is that this declaration was not recognized by Thai envoys in the United States and Great Britain, where the *Free Thai* movement was formed. It eventually became a part of the allied efforts in the conflict.

1942

The Japanese International Tourism Bureau requested that the ***Imperial Hotel*** *in Tokyo take over the management of The Oriental.*

Japanese armed forces requisitioned The Oriental. The average occupancy was 25 guests per night. In February 1942 the Japanese International Tourism Bureau requested that the Imperial Hotel, the most prestigious in Tokyo, take over the management of The Oriental. The Imperial duly sent four employees, headed by Mankichi Sugiyama, The Oriental's new general manager. During the war years the Imperial Hotel managed various hotel properties in conquered territories throughout Asia, among them the Goodwood Park in Singapore, the Strand in Burma and the Brastagi Heights Hotel in Sumatra.

In 1943 American forces began a major counter-offensive in the Pacific. The United States regained their superiority and it became clear that American forces were heading for Okinawa and eventually for the Japanese mainland.

¤

In 1969 **Alec Waugh**, *the English novelist and travel writer* (Where the Clock Chimes Twice, Island in the Sun), *returned to Bangkok. He was shocked by the rapid changes that had taken place throughout the city. His taxi slowly approached the hotel:*

'We turned to the right, then to the left. My heart contracted. Whatever else had changed, I prayed that The Oriental would be the same. My prayer was granted. No first-class hotel has a less prepossessing exterior.

... Within a few minutes I was looking down from the third-floor window on to the green lawn, the palm trees and the old, two storied facade with the words "Oriental Hotel" in antique lettering.

... in front of it were the two classical statues carrying lamps, just as they had been when Maugham suffered from the fever ...'

1946

1960s

The oldest part of The Oriental is today known as the Author's Wing. It was opened in 1887 and origianlly housed the lobby, the bar and the restaurant with its kitchens. All the guest-rooms were located upstairs.

Krull

Sanuk

Business

Changes

The year was 1946: Bhumibol Adulyadej, the present king, became the ninth monarch of the Chakkri dynasty.

The war was over and the grand old lady Oriental, with calm resignation, carried on her role as hostess, giving a little sigh now and again about her forsaken garden, her threadbare carpets, her dusty floor and broken furniture. After the war American armed forces had requisitioned The Oriental. What little remained did overtime duty when it accommodated women and children evacuated from Japanese prison camps in Java. The Oriental housed liberated Dutch, British and Australian prisoners of war. Some of the ex-prisoners regarded tableware and linen as Japanese property and years later some of it could still be found in Bangkok's thieves' market. The manageress was Maria Robins from England. The hotel had seven suites, 24 regular rooms with baths and 10 small rooms left.

Around this time Germaine Krull, a French photo-journalist, took over the running of the hotel. Her partners were Colonel Jim Thompson, the future founder of the Thai Silk Co, General Chai Prateepasen, HRH Prince Bhanu, Mr Pote Sarasin and Mr John Wester. Thompson lived at the hotel.

Germaine was busy restoring life to this

remarkable institution, such as organising a complete spring clean of the building, repainting and rewiring, finding out how the water system worked and dealing with a lot of other prosaic yet essential tasks. But despite temperamental electricity and an erratic water supply, the hotel was filled to the very last room with guests of every kind, from fortune hunters to diplomats.

Germaine Krull, *out of a job, subsequently found herself in charge of the day-to-day running of Bangkok's most famous hostelry.*

Germaine brought in the age of post-war grandeur at The Oriental, still *the* hotel in the city. With the opening of the Bamboo Bar she established Bangkok's most fashionable hangout. It became the great 'sanuk' (fun) place, where people often stood six and seven deep at the bar and where sometimes on Saturday night guests had 'sanuk' until four in the morning, dancing and singing in the manner and style of many different nationalities.

After humble beginnings as a tiny room filled with mosquitoes, it was made larger, refurbished and given a simple, generous, attractive French–American menu. Croissants and brioches were available in the morning, hamburgers or hot dogs for lunch, table d'hôte and à la carte at any time.

Germaine Krull's Agence des Presses decided to close down its photo agency. Krull's assignment was consequently terminated and she found alternative employment in charge of the day-to-day running of Bangkok's most famous hostelry. Here are some highlights of her humorous account.

'For opening the Bamboo Bar I began to plan a reception, but the number of people we could crowd in was definitely limited. So I decided to have several parties, a Rotarian luncheon being first on the list. All the guests turned up and were enthusiastic.

'I chose the best boys and cooks of the staff for the bar. There was a special barbecue kitchen behind a window where people could see the food being prepared. I planned to serve only grilled food and sandwiches with a petite marmite and spring chicken as specialities.

'I did not know how American sandwiches, hamburgers and cheeseburgers should taste, so I could not teach the cook. I was lucky, though, because an American couple who were both lawyers, Mr and Mrs Al Lyman, were staying at the hotel. Frieda Lyman agreed readily to instruct the cook how to prepare American sandwiches and show the boys how they should be served. It took most of her vitality and determination before she overcame the cook's resistance and got him to produce what she wanted. Added to that, she had to find a bakery that would make the kind of bread that was needed for sandwiches and buns for hamburgers and cheeseburgers. Ph.D.s from the Hanoi University had painted our walls and repaired our furniture, princesses had sewn sheets, and now we had a brilliant

American lawyer from Washington, D.C., to teach our cooks to make hamburgers.

The Bamboo Bar is the *place for having* **sanuk**, *the friendly Thai expression for* ***fun***.

'The first evening passed off smoothly enough, but by the second day the pianist announced that he would not be able to come again. Our Bamboo Bar was open and we had no musicians. Lerm searched the city and finally turned up with a Thai pianist, but he and the girl musician started quarrelling immediately. He resented the number of ashtrays she threw at him and wanted to leave. She also threw ashtrays at the guests if she did not like the way they looked at her. As people can dance to drums and a trumpet, even if no ashtrays are thrown, we decided to dispense with the energetic girl.

'To give the Bamboo Bar an atmosphere of elegance I thought the least our guests could do would be to wear a tie. If anyone arrived without, we gave him one. We made hundreds of ties with the cheapest satin and the children of the Chinese boys painted cocks on them. These ties went round the world as they were collected by visitors and local guests. I bought the most hideous colours I could find. But still, no one objected to wearing a garish orange tie while his partner might be beautifully dressed in pink Thai silk.

Running The Oriental

¤

A list of some of the varied individuals who have managed the hotel.
Owners appear in parantheses.

¤

1863 (?) Captain James White
1878 H Jarck (C Salje)
1887 Georges Troisoeufs (Messrs Andersen & Co)
1890 Mr Allen
April 1891 Mr Smith
September 1891 George F Kornloff
1893 W J Palmer (Franklin 'Bill' Hurst)
1899 (a syndicate represented by a Mr W Downie)
1903 F S Robertson
1904 Carl G Edwards (Mme M O Bujault)
1910 Mme Maria Maire
1932 Lt. Col and Mrs Sylow
1935 Mr J O Hossig
1940 Maria Robins
1942 Mankichi Sugiyama
1945 Maria Robins
1947 Germaine Krull
(Germaine Krull, Jim Thompson, Chai Prateepasen,
Prince Bhanu, Pote Sarasin, John Wester)
1960 Robert Fassom
1963 Barrie Cross
1965 Albert Urscheler
1967 Kurt Wachtveitl
(Italthai–Hong Kong Land, from 1972)

'One morning an elegant lady approached me: "Oh, my dear, I am so very happy to meet you. You know this place was formerly my father-in-law's palace. You see, I met my husband in England and it was actually King Edward who introduced him to me."

'My eyes must have got rounder and rounder and I think she noticed, because she continued, "Yes, I see you don't know much about the olden days. My husband's father was sent by King Rama the Fifth to Europe to establish what we would call an embassy today. My husband was born and brought up abroad, and lived like a high ranking prince at the Court of St. James. The middle of your hotel was his father's palace. All the land where the Chartered Bank and the French Legation are located on one side and the East Asiatic and Assumption College on the other belonged to my father-in-law and he gave it away to the foreigners just like that. My husband was the one who built the big wing which your guests call 'bowling alley'. His father only gave him permission to build it after a long struggle because the idea of an hotel was repugnant to him. But my husband thought we had to do something for the poor foreign captains and sailors who came to Siam and did not know where to stay."

"The middle of your hotel was his father's palace."

"All the land belonged to my father-in-law and he gave it away to the foreigners just like that."

'On she went like a waterfall, "I am so happy to see you have made it such a nice place. I always loved it even though I only saw it once or twice. You see, my husband spent most of his life in England. and when I first came here with him this place was already a hotel. I am so glad to meet you."

'Two Russian girls, who had been friends of rich Europeans in Shanghai, arrived with this group [of Chinese fleeing the Communists] and moved into the hotel. Ann, of course, had taken them for fine ladies and accepted their booking. I was not very happy to have them as no bachelor was safe from them as long as he was willing to pay their bar bills and they made my bar their scene of operations.

'One morning Kim, the no.1, came to my office and asked, "Mem, we do not allow Masters to bring lady friends into their rooms after nine o' clock. What happens when a Mem brings Masters into her room? Is that O.K.?"

"What do you mean, Kim?" I asked.

" Well, every morning Mem from no. 24 and from no. 25 have Master from no. 12, Master from no. 26, and Master from no.41 coming to their rooms and even sleeping there till next morning. Oh, Mem no. 24 is very beautiful when she is dressed, but in the morning . . . oh . . . oh."

"All right, Kim. I will look after this. You do not have to say anything more." Mem no. 24 and Mem no. 25 made a lot of noise and angry protests when I told them I needed their rooms

Swimming pools were not always part of the basic facilities of an Asian hotel. The Oriental got its first pool only after World War II but its location was always unsatisfactory. Eventually Giorgio Berlingieri decided to dig two pools as they are today.

and could not keep them. It took all my diplomacy to transfer them to another hotel where life would be easier for them. They did not stay in Bangkok long, however. One day an import-export man took them away with him to fields better suited to their talents.

'Our bill collectors had their problems. One debtor had left the French Embassy as an address and, when the collector called there, he was said never to have been there, but the officials were able to give him the man's address. He called at the home and was given a sealed envelope which he brought in, assuming that it contained money. On opening it Ruang found the following extraordinary letter which he brought to me:

Dear Madam,

I received your letter of yesterday's date. I am very sorry with the attitude shown me, especially when I am born the greatest Super human the world has ever known.

Didn't you know dear Madam that by act of God and Nature and my parents I am created a super natural at Silom, Bangrak on the Monday, 28th September, 1896, at 7 a.m.

Well let me tell you in this letter and by law of nature that a super natural need not have any money.

If you think I have to pay for the meals and etc. incurred in the Oriental Hotel you may with my greatest pleasure report my matter to the High Commission of Police of Thailand Nai Phow Sri Yanon or the highest authority in the country.

I wish to thank you very much here for your kindness and remember that kindness shall be returned for kindness and nothing else.

With nothing further but wish you good health, peace, happiness and prosperity and may God bless you and your family,

Yours sincerely,
H.W. Berlandier
Thai Super Natural Extraordinary.

The Lobby *in the fifties. Now ceiling fans did the job of the Punkah wallahs. Air-conditioning was not yet installed.*

"What are we going to do with this?" asked Ruang.

"I never agreed to be responsible for supernatural beings in the hotel," I replied.

'The vogue for wanting things they couldn't have or which didn't belong to them was not confined to the hotel staff but extended to hotel guests. A Thai ashtray seldom remained in the hotel longer than a day. If we began the evening with five ashtrays on the bar, there were none left when it closed.

'All the little bells, which were difficult to get, disappeared from the tables. I imported novel wooden pepper mills from abroad but they became so popular with the guests and their appearances on the tables so brief, that I gave up on ordering them.

'I went to a great deal of trouble to have special lamps made for the tables in the Bamboo Bar. The bases were carved teak elephants about six inches high. The shades were of hide with cut-out Thai designs of flowers or animals. We only retained them because the boys knew the customers most likely to walk off with them and did not hesitate to check in the late evening hours.

'There were times when I felt I was carrying a leaking bucket, what with money disappearing like magic into the pockets of charming employees and hotel equipment spirited away by equally charming guests.'

Life had returned to normal. Bangkok became re-established as a destination of international travellers. Mrs Eleanore Roosevelt arrived in 1950 as guest of the Thai government to speak at the American Association luncheon held at The Oriental, where a crowd of over a thousand people awaited her.

In 1958 Germaine Krull's great achievement, the Tower Wing, opened. While it was under construction one of her partners in the business, Mr Pote Sarasin, became Prime Minister of Thailand.

'Having one of my partners as premier was no advantage,' Germaine comments, 'as he was fully occupied at a time when I needed advice for the many problems. The floors were already almost fully occupied when the lifts were installed at last and the official opening date was set to be the 1st of April. I sent out the invitations telling my friends it was not an April Fool's joke but the lucky date chosen by a famous old monk.'

In November of the same year Le Normandie restaurant opened on the top floor of the new tower wing, featuring a Norman-style chimney-piece topped by two rampant lions, emblem of Normandy.

Germaine had stumbled upon them in the thieves' market. A superb view was offered by the enormous picture windows down both long sides of the room, showing the river on one side and metropolitan Bangkok on the other. A *Bangkok Post* article commented: 'Probably the best location for tourists of any restaurant in the whole of Bangkok, and combined with good food and service this roof-top establishment is deservedly the first place that residents usually take their visitors from overseas for a meal.'

In April 1967 Jim Thompson, founder of the Thai Silk Company and part owner of The Oriental disappeared amid mysterious circumstances in the highlands of Malaysia.

This brings an end to an era. And it is the start of the modern epoch, when a new generation of businessmen took over the fabled old hotel.

~

1966
A royal visit

The Oriental had the honour to welcome Her Majesty, Queen Sirikit, who presided over the opening of the Rotary Bazaar held at the hotel.

La Crème de la Cuisine

two atmospheric shots of Le Normandie Grill and the Thai dance show at the Sala Rim Naam across the river. At both restaurants exquisit cuisine surpasses every expectation. At Le Normandie a visiting three-star chef from France is almost a regualr treat.

Berlingieri

Old Tradition — Modern Times

1967 — 1980

River Wing

Wachtveitl

Pool

hen businessmen take over an enterprise as promising as the Oriental Hotel one would imagine that facts and figures are all important. Not with The Oriental. Here management skills must be combined with a big heart. One of the most important players in the life of The Oriental, luckily, had both. He was a man of 'first-class brains, a generous heart and on top of this great combination a sense of humour to go with it' as Kurt Wachtveitl, longest-serving general manager of The Oriental, lovingly recalls him.

Giorgio Berlingieri, born in Genoa in Italy in 1922, entered The Oriental's history book in 1967. His company Italthai was well on the way to becoming one of country's most significant mercantile groups, eventually comprising over 60 companies, covering almost all aspects of the Thai economy. Italthai was founded in the mid-fifties by Giorgio Berlingieri as a joint-venture with Dr Chaijudh Karnasuta. This very Dr Karnasuta first called Berlingieri about The Oriental in 1967. Berlingieri later reproduced this conversation in *An Oriental Album:**

* **An Oriental Album** *is out of print. It was written in the late seventies with the help of, among others, Mrs Chancham. She helped again on the research for this book. To preserve the spirit and authenticity of the* Album *we have made use of its material as much as possible in this book.*

'The first step leading to the acquisition was taken in mid-air, so to speak. My partner, Dr Chaijudh Karnasuta, co-chairman of the Italthai, put in a long-distance call to me, as I was on a business trip to Italy.

"There's a hotel for sale."

"Forget it," was my immediate reply.

"It's The Oriental Hotel," said Dr Chaijudh, a man of few words.

"Why didn't you say so?" I cried. "Of course, we'll buy it!"

"That's what I thought you would say," the good doctor calmly remarked.

And that was that.'

Chancham Bunnag

One of the many good spirits of The Oriental. Involved in the writing of An Oriental Album in the late 1970s she helped again on the research for this book.

Berlingieri, an expert frogman, dived into new, unknown waters. He was a graduate of naval and mechanical engineering with full marks from the University of Genoa. His work concentrated on ship salvage, clearing ships wrecked during the war. He was based first in Vietnam (where he met his wife Mimi) and eventually on the Chao Phraya River.

If this seems an unlikely background there was another side to the Italian who appeared 'a gentleman all the way, toujours avec son cigare', as Peter Bunnag put it in Berlingieri's obituary book.* The connoisseur of fine wines, the founder of the Bangkok Gourmet Club and the 'man with something more' as Charles Regnault, his assistant for over ten years, put it, Berlingieri had his own understanding of a grand hotel. His plans went beyond the horizon of the City of Angels. His aim was clear: The Oriental must become one of the best hotels in the world.

Berlingieri was far too busy with his various businesses (Nipa Lodge, a beach hotel; the

** It is a tradition in Thailand to produce a book on the life of celebrated individuals after their death.*

Berlingieri & Bocuse

L'important c'est la cuisine Paul Bocuse 8/2 1977

Berlingieri had his own ideas about restaurants: 'People always judge the hotel by its restaurants. He was right. A born gourmet like many Italians, Berlingieri's knowledge of food and wine was excellent. It appears extraordinary that there was no spaghetti on the menu. Berlingieri explained that spaghetti should be cooked "al dente" with split-second timing, a task too difficult to perform in a restaurant.'

Bangkok World, a newspaper; Siam Bricks, a factory producing hollow bricks from clay; Ital-Lao, his first venture outside Thailand) to take charge personally. He looked instead for an able lieutenant to run the hotel for him. Two years previously Surin, his secretary, had recommended a man she had met as a student in Switzerland to manage the Nipa Lodge in Pattaya. Later, in November 1967, Berlingieri said to this man: 'Why don't you go to Bangkok and do some work for a change?'

The tall, slim man was Kurt Wachtveitl, an individualist from head to foot.

Giorgio's widow, the late Mimi Berlingieri, later recalled the special bond between these two men: 'They were not like son and father as my husband was too young to be his father, but he was like a guiding friend to Kurt.'

Kurt Wachtveitl looks back respectfully: 'He was extremely critical about the hotel's restaurants. So his first step was to change the Normandie Grill.

"People always judge the hotel by its restaurants," Berlingieri said. He was right. Although the guest-rooms were a little outmoded at this time, by January 1969, people were flocking again and again to the little inn by the river of the kings. A born gourmet like all Italians, Berlingieri's knowledge of food and wine was excellent. It appears extraordinary that there was no spaghetti on the menu. Berlingieri explained that spaghetti should be cooked "al dente" with split-second timing, a task too difficult to perform in a restaurant.'

When down-to-earth Mimi with her entrepreneurial husband Giorgio Berlingieri, the young and motivated Kurt Wachtveitl and his elegant wife Khun Penny teamed up, the hotel possessed an irresistible driving force that would lead it to international renown.

In the 1970s rooms at The Oriental cost 275 baht for a single and 390 baht for a double. The Royal and Thai suites in the old building were 1,000 baht per night. At this point the owners of the Mandarin Hotel in Hong Kong decided to establish Mandarin International Hotels Ltd and expand into South-East Asia. The Oriental matched their requirements in Thailand. The two companies entered into a partnership in 1972 which continues harmoniously to this day. The story of the deal was recounted by Berlingieri in *An Oriental Album* (see pages 118–120).

The oldest part of the hotel, the Authors' Wing, was another target for extensive renovations. Only a few months after they were completed on Monday, 13 August 1973, a fire damaged the historic wing. Misfortune spelt challenge for Berlingieri. Even before the fire engines had retreated he stood in the debris of smouldering teak wood, calmly assessed the damage and then announced the date for the reopening of this much-loved part of the hotel.

Kurt Wachtveitl

a man with a vision. He graduated from the hotel school at Lausanne, Switzerland in 1961, read history of art and literature in Rome, Italy and philosophy in Spain. He married his Thai girlfriend against all odds. He still cuts his own hair. Professional career: Trois Couronnes, Vevey; Beau-Rivage Palace, Lausanne (where he met his wife Penny); Suvretta Haus, St Moritz; Park Lane Hilton, London.

The good doctor Chaijudh Karnasuta who suggested: 'There is a hotel for sale . . .'

The next day a team of workers from Italthai arrived to start restoring the Author's Wing to its former glory.

It was also time to replace the Ambassador Wing which had served as the 'modern' extension of Germaine Krull's Tower Wing. It had done its duty. In 1976 the new River Wing was completed although the siting of the swimming pools still troubled the Oriental team.

Two small pools had been embedded in the extensive lawns. The one in front of the coffee shop was fine, but the one in front of the Author's Wing had to be moved. While searching for the perfect location many ideas were proposed. None really worked until one day Berlingieri and Wachtveitl stood in the Normandie Grill and looked down on the hotel grounds: 'That's the spot,' Berlingieri said, pointing at the place where the pool is today. 'That's the spot for our new pool.'

'That's the spot for our new pool.' (Giorgio Berlingieri)

GIORGIO BERLINGIERI *personally recalled the creation of the partnership with Mandarin Hotels in his book* AN ORIENTAL ALBUM:

'In refurbishing the Tower Wing, we turned our attention to another main section of the hotel, the Ambassador Wing; and the more we contemplated it the more dissatisfied we became. Apart from their general state of obsolescence (among other things the air-conditioning system had about reached the point of no return), the rooms let you down in one other respect: they were so close to the river yet lay at such an angle that they barely commanded any view of it. All in all the whole building lacked the discreet charm of the old Oriental, and it was up to us to put it right.

'At this same period, while debating what course to take, we had the opportunity to buy the land of the old Chartered Bank which had been the Oriental's practically next-door neighbour for some eighty years. The purchase eventually took place and the extra space allowed us to plan something dramatic not only for the wing but for the Oriental as a whole.

'However, if a small hotel can be successfully operated in an independent, family-business sort of way, it is hardly the case for a 400-room establishment. We started looking for partners. We had preliminary talks with international chains and airlines that led to nothing. The project, for various reasons, was considered too risky by these concerns. Then our luck turned. Through our good friends at the Hong

The Oriental of Krull and Thompson: the Tower Wing is completed, to the left the Ambassador Wing.

The early 1970s. The Ambassador Wing is still in use, while to the left the new River Wing is underway.

Kong and Shanghai Banking Corporation we were introduced to the Hong Kong Land people. It was love at first sight, a veritable coup de foudre. *They were expanding the Mandarin into the leading international hotels chain in South-East Asia, and the Oriental matched their exacting requirements for Thailand. Our quest came to an end. Here was the partner we had been searching for.*

'After two telexed messages, I met Mullan Cunningham of the Mandarin International Hotels Ltd., and in the record time of 35 minutes we reached an agreement which was later finalised in a legal form without a single change in substance. In Vernon Roberts, managing director of Hong Kong Land, we found an ideal collaborator, one who was making decisions at least as fast as we could propose them. Drawings for the extension were worked out in due course, capital was increased to Baht 100 million, additional loan was raised, the first piles were driven and we were on our way to making the 1970's another exciting decade for The Oriental.

Vernon Roberts, managing director of Hong Kong Land, 'who was making decisions at least as fast as we could propose them.'

'Messrs F. Jarck and C. Salje – those Falstaffian hosts at the beginning of our story – would have

As the River Wing nears completion, the old Ambassador Wing is demolished. Slowly the Oriental Hotel takes on its present appearance.

been amazed at the latest extensions of the Oriental Hotel, though probably not for long. As exponents of the bold and adventurous they could take the most astounding things in their stride; they would have gaped at the River Wing, then chuckled and let out hearty cheers of approbation before settling down to do justice to all the new delights their old place now had to offer. They would have felt at home, for despite the efficiency – something they never paid much attention to – the innovations, the technological advances and all that, it is still the same old bubbling unstinting spirit of friendliness and hospitality that pervades and holds sway over everything, just as it did in their days.

'The 350-room River Wing, completed in 1976, stands as testimony to the amicable and mutually beneficial partnership of the Italthai Company and the Mandarin International Hotels Ltd. (affiliate of Hong Kong Land Co. Ltd.).'

•

*To the right:
Night over Bangkok: the illuminated River Wing with it's lovely corner suites. On the first floor Lord Jim's restaurant, in front the River Terrace.*

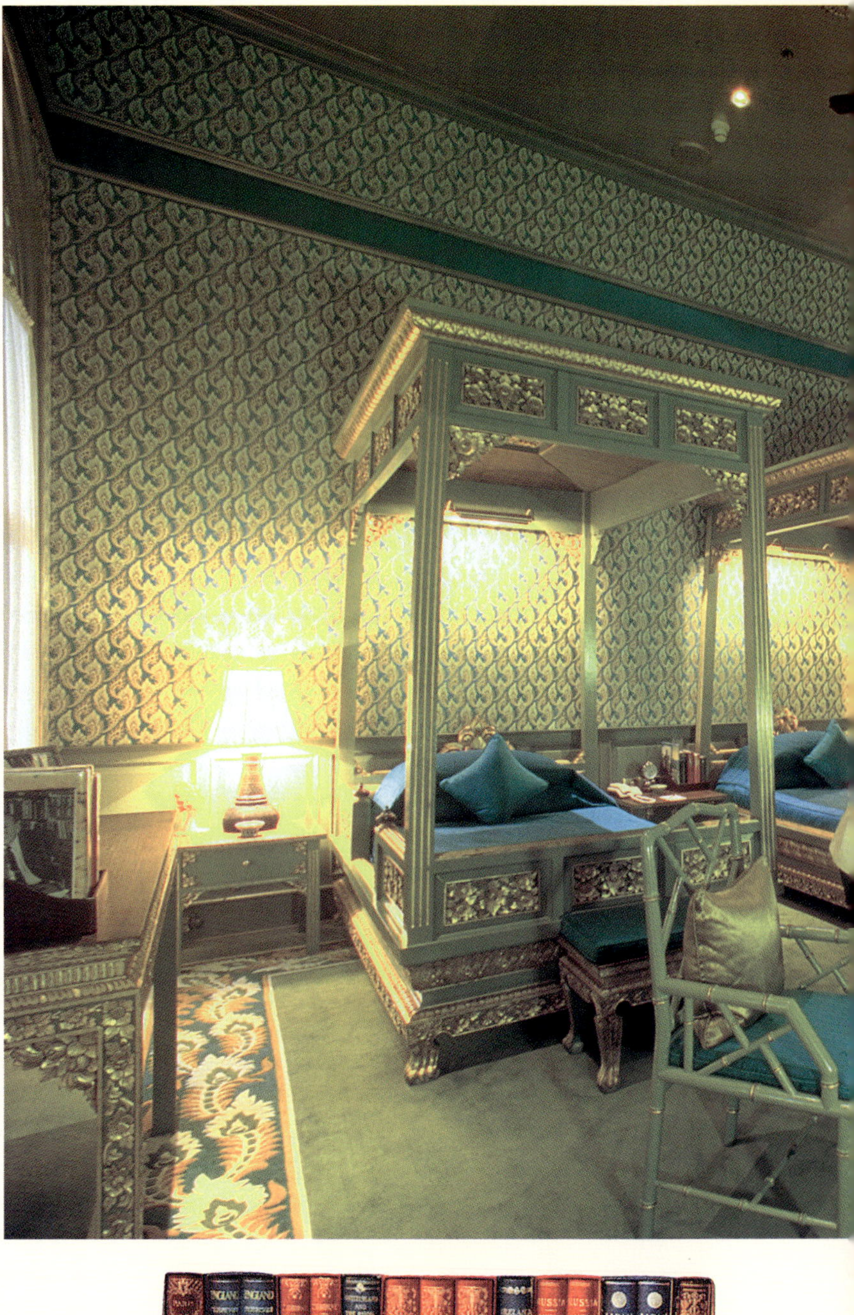

ENGLAND
ENGLAND
RUSSIA
RUSSIA
JAPAN
AND
HER PEOPLE
JAPAN
AND
HER PEOPLE

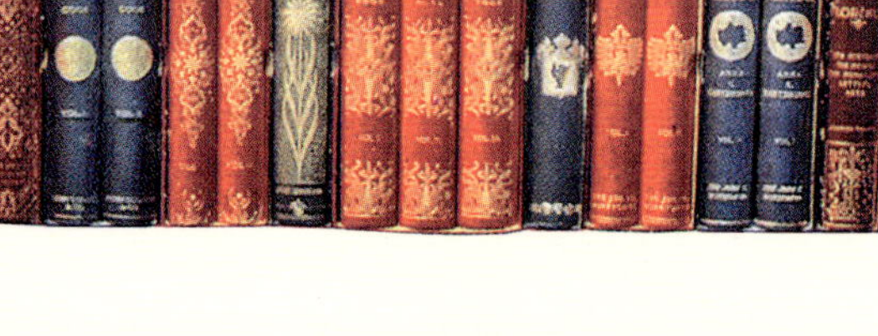

THE NOËL COWARD SUITE

in the author's wing – together with the Somerset Maugham Suite – is one of the most famous haunts for the discerning traveller in Asia. While Conrad never slept at the hotel Maugham was a regular visitor to The Oriental.

Enquiries
SIGNING CONTRACT

A HOTEL IS OPERATED BY PEOPLE. THESE PEOPLE MATTER MORE THAN ALL THE MACHINES, LIMOUSINES AND RIVER LAUNCHES. MACHINES DO NOT TALK. THE SECRET LIES IN A FRIENDLY WORD AND A SMILE.

Members of The Oriental's executive staff surround the late Mimi Berlingieri (centre, left of manager Kurt Wachtveitl). She was an active director of the hotel until her death in 1995.

1980

–

TODAY

Left page:

Any Enquiries – who would hesitate to ask? ◊ Preparing a signboard in the lobby

Everything goes with a friendly smile ◊ Dancing beauty at the Sala Rim Naam show ◊ Sanuk - the Thai word for fun - is obviously part of the work

You do not need to tip the carver ◊ The biggest smile cannot hide the fact that Thai oranges taste like mandarins ◊ Chef at the breakfast buffet on the terrace

The river launch busily crosses the Chao Phraya River between the main building of the hotel and the Sala Rim Naam, the Oriental Spa and the Thai cooking school ◊ Ice carvers at work - they sculpture pieces of art every day.

There are 977 Thais and 11 non-Asians working at The Oriental.

In 1981 the spotlight of worldwide recognition suddenly changed to the limelight of international applause. The American bankers' magazine *Institutional Investor* voted the Oriental Hotel in Bangkok the best hotel in the world. The world press joined in the singing. The effect was tremendous. Journalists from all over the globe flocked to this highly praised temple of hospitality. Travellers would rather give up their ticket home than miss out on experiencing a cup of tea on The Oriental's terrace.

Berlingieri, the far-sighted entrepreneur, died in his office on the morning of 1 December 1981. He had seen his dream come true. *His* Oriental was the number one hotel in the world. Business boomed. The 1980s were to be a golden age.

Wachtveitl* continued to strive for excellence. His respect for the historic background of the hotel led to the conclusion, our history is our future.

A hotelier and philosopher, he knew that happy customers are the best job security. If he did not take care of his guests, somebody else in this vibrating and fast-developing city would. He introduced the simplest but most powerful rule of the hospitality trade: always give people more than they expect to get.

New hotels opened in Bangkok. Many offered accommodation at below market prices and yet

* **Kurt Wachtveitl** *became* Boss of the Year 1981, *as nominated by the Women Secretaries' Association of Thailand. In 1987 he was awarded the Cross of the Order of Merit of the Federal Republic of Germany for 20 years of outstanding work for the renowned hotel. In Thailand he was given the Royal Decoration of Fourth Class (Companion) of The Most Exalted Order of the White Elephant in appreciation of his work in the travel industry.*

despite this fierce competition The Oriental continued to thrive. It had survived its first century without ever questioning its reputation as the best address in Bangkok.

In 1983 the *Sala Rim Naam* Thai restaurant celebrated its opening with a dinner for over 200 guests. New suites and rooms at The Oriental assured the international traveller of the latest state-of-the-art accommodation, be it in mattresses or tele-communications. Refurbishing 100 rooms in one season was a matter of course during the eighties. Newly created suites were named after eminent figures in the world of arts and culture with links to the hotel including: the late M R Kukrit Pramoj, Thailand's prominent man of politics, literature and affairs of state, regular guest and author Gore Vidal, Somerset Maugham, Noël Coward, Joseph Conrad and Graham Greene.

Resident Manager Jonas A. Schuermann takes care of a dear guest; Sir Peter Ustinov.

The Oriental Suite was refurbished at a cost of approximately US$500,000. Its style is like a summer palace built at the turn of the century. The grand entrance hall features imported Georgian hand-cut crystal chandeliers, silvery white marble floor and a carpet of intricate symmetrical pattern. Silk wall coverings, teak floors and rugs are everywhere, all specially created, each designed to refreshingly

Oriental Suite
the master bedroom with its hand-painted design on the ceiling.

harmonise with the tropical flora and fauna of the country. All this comes with a view of the Chao Phraya, one of the most fascinating along the river. The master bedroom has a four-poster bed and a hand-painted design on the ceiling which complements the general design of the room. The guest bedroom – who wants to be alone in such extravagance – is as well-appointed as the main bedroom. The dining-room across the gallery, also with a superb river view, is the ideal place for leisurely meals. Just ask your personal butler what's cooking.

In 1980, for the sake of posterity, the Louis T Leonowens Time Capsule was sealed in front of the old Authors' Wing in the concrete base of the company's symbol, a huge swing. Dr Thanat Khoman, deputy prime minister, was the guest of honour who placed and sealed the capsule. It contains artefacts of the present, photographs, newspapers and some little secrets which will only be revealed when the capsule is opened in 75 years time on 5 June 2055.

Having reached the zenith of technological sophistication, The Oriental has never failed to concentrate on its old strength: the human factor. A hotel is operated by people. These people matter more than all the machines, limousines and river launches. Machines do not talk. The secret lies in a friendly word and a smile. The attitudes and behaviour of almost 1,000 staff (977 Thais and 11 non-Asians, to be precise) were the daily concern and, quite

***Robert Rauschenberg** left this piece of art in the guestbook during his visit to The Oriental in 1983*

possibly, headache of former personnel manager Weena Sornchai. How do you deal with unhappiness, selfishness and the inevitable conflicts of so many service personnel? Western ideas of team spirit, interpersonal relationships and stress management have been tried but found to be only partially successful. So The Oriental has turned to the psychological observations of Dr Oat Vareeraksh of Chiang Mai University and Phra Buddhadasa Bhiku's Buddhist teaching. This means regular retreats for groups of staff to Suan Mokh Monastery in Surat Thani for four days of discussions, lectures and meditation.

'Afterwards a notable difference in people's behaviour is observable,' says Khun Weena. From the front desk to waiters and waitresses, duties are performed with pleasure and a smile.

Rabieb Boonkuncheing

is manageress of the hotel's telephone exchange. She was bombarded with calls when Michael Jackson stayed at the hotel. The star did not want to be disturbed, so whenever a caller asked to be put through to him, Khun Rabieb coped by impersonating him. She switched the caller to another line, cooing 'I love you all' in a high-pitched American accent. It would be interesting to know how many people in Bangkok believe that Michael Jackson has actually spoken to them!

Love always
Michael Jackson

Ankana Kalantananda *is undoubtedly the longest-serving employee. She was the first Thai woman to enter the hotel business and went to Paris to train. Khun Ankana has worked for six managers. She is part of more than one third of the 120 years of history. As one can see she enjoyed the 120 years anniversary party on 22 January 1996 very much (below, dancing with Peter Marriott)*

It is yet another secret behind the hotel's success.

The Oriental launched an apprenticeship programme (OHAP) for 100 young people every year. Plans are also underway to create, in cooperation with the prestigious hotel school in Lausanne, Switzerland, an equally comprehensive hotel school in Thailand.

Some of the staff have spent the greater part of their lives in service at The Oriental. Look at Khun Ankana. She celebrated 45 years with the hotel in 1992. She joined the hotel when Germaine Krull was the manager. She recalls with great humour the days of mosquito nets and no running hot water. A deluxe room then depended on the thickness of the *kapok* mattresses and the quality of the mosquito nets. Old guests treasure the warm welcome and know The Oriental is still the same when Khun Ankana greets them. But the driving forces backstage never rest. A typical year's calendar might read as follows.

January: annual Thank You party for the hotel's supporters. March: guest performance of La Tour d'Argent of Paris at the Normandie. May: Eight of the best chefs appear at Le Normandie. June: The Savoy, London presents afternoon tea in the Authors' Lounge. July: Italian Seafood and Pasta Festival featuring Giannino, Milan's oldest eatery at Lord Jim's. August: Indonesia Week at Lord Jim's. Grouse Festival at Le Normandie with Anton Mosiman.

September: Thai theatre production of My Fair Lady; *3-star Belgian chef Pierre Romeyer at Le Normandie; Leonard Paris; International Fashion show; SEA Write Awards. October: 3-star chef Georges Blanc at Le Normandie. November: 3-star chefs Jacques and Alain Pic at Le Normandie; Loy Krathong Night; Mozart in concert featuring The Festival Strings, Lucerne. December: The Oriental's famous Christmas and New Year's Eve parties.*

Celebrating a wedding at The Oriental has been an integral part of Bangkok life for over 100 years.

In 1992 The Oriental opened the first Oriental Shop at Bangkok's Isetan shopping complex. In 1995 a second Oriental Shop was opened at the Lake Rajada office complex selling gift items, fine chocolates, pâtés, wines and almost everything needed for an exquisite gourmet dinner at home.

When in Thailand ...

At The Oriental you can learn how to cook Thai food. The Oriental Thai cooking school is situated opposite the hotel on the other side of the river.

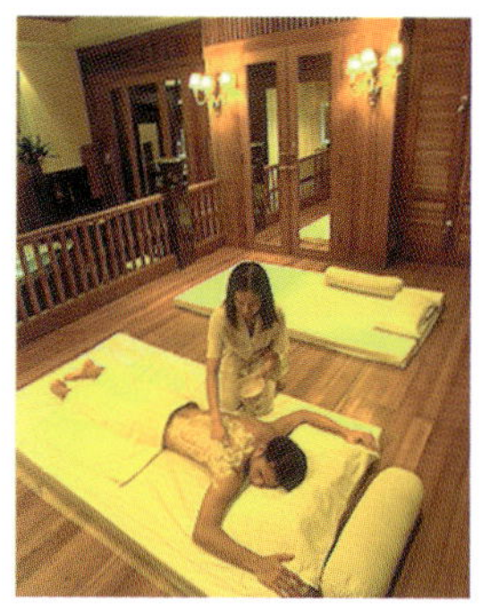

The Oriental Spa *offers specialised massage therapies, European skin care, hydrotherapy, aroma therapy and Balneotherm body treatments, Swiss showers, steam rooms and saunas, yoga, stress management, nutrition counselling and behavioural modification.*

The *Oriental Queen* *Over one million passengers have made the trip upstream on the daily river cruise to the ancient capital of Ayutthaya.*

In 1993 the one millionth passenger on *The Oriental Queen*'s daily river cruise to the ancient capital of Ayutthaya stepped aboard. The same year saw the opening of The Oriental Spa, a Thai health and beauty centre, a completely new concept in Thailand, costing US$5 million. Aiming at the ultimate in revitalisation for the body, mind and spirit, it is uniquely Thai both in its surroundings and in its approach to treatment and service.

All the hotel's kitchens are under the experienced supervision of executive chef Norbert A Kostner from South Tyrol. They are worth their own book. Chef Norbert has a lot of stories to tell. Ask him about the African President who brought his own chefs to prepare fresh frogs every day.

One ton of freshly squeezed oranges, 150 kg of rock-lobster, 10,000 pieces of bread, 600 breakfasts and up to 5,000 meals leave the kitchen every day. These are impressive figures when considered next to chef Norbert's belief that 'our main problem is that we often have to feed people who are not really hungry.'

There is also the French restaurant Le Normandie. Its inspired menu is the creation of Michelin 3-star consultant chef Alain Senderens and his protégé Frederic Heba. It is a dining experience that is as much a privilege as it is a pleasure. Once a year La Tour d'Argent celebrates a festival of *cuisine extraordinaire* on the top floor of the old wing. La Tour d'Argent is the oldest Parisian restaurant dating back to 1582. Tradition has it that Henri III ate there and used a fork for the first time. About 100 years ago they had the idea of attributing a serial number to each duck that was served. For several years now The Oriental has issued numbers too and each spring Bangkok society gathers around the famous ducks while the staff of La Tour d'Argent literally squeezes the maximum out of each bird. Seven hundred kilos of ducks are flown in from France every year.

Only the best chefs of the world give guest performances at The Oriental. Very recently Joel Robuchon and Jean-Claude Vrinat worked together in The Oriental kitchen.

Chef Norbert Kostner

All kitchens are under the experienced supervision of executive chef Norbert A Kostner from South Tyrol who, on special occasions, even confides secret recipes to special guests.

HM Queen Elizabeth visited Bangkok in 1996 and enjoyed the cooking of Norbert Kostner's team tremendously.

The visit of **La Tour d'Argent** *every year is a regular culinary highlight in the city. With 700 kilos of duck breasts the silver press (left) gets busy.*

Epilogue

The hotel never sleeps. No day is typical. Early one particular morning there is an annual ceremony when directors and staff members of various departments of the hotel hand over food offerings to monks, one for each year of the hotel's official age. The ceremony is convivial and joyous. Wachtveitl, for example, does it with a smile, with Thai *sanuk*, the art of fun and pleasure. An old monk receives an apple from him, nods his head and blesses him: Wachtveitl smiles and says: 'An apple a day keeps the doctor away.'

An apple a day keeps the doctor away!

Once a year, early in the morning, 122 monks – one for each year of the hotel's official age – line up to receive the traditional food offerings.

Later in the day the hotel's Honesty Award is presented to a member of staff. Returned diamond rings are routine for the hotel's front office. A food promotion adds another funny story to the diary of the hotel. The fixed-price lunch buffet proclaims: 'Eat as much as you can.' One guest makes the most of it. He eats, falls asleep, wakes up and eats again.

Afternoon tea in the Author's Lounge is accompanied by gentle music. Behind the wall in the hotel's exclusive library time appears to stand still. There Madam Ankana presides over books, photographs and memorabilia.

At the two swimming pools sun worshippers relax after sightseeing. On the terrace visitors watch the life on the river over their first drink of the day. The *Oriental Queen* returns from her daily

TO :

Q8

FROM :

- [ ] For your information
- [ ] For your comments
- [ ] For your signature
- [ ] For your approval
- [ ] Please handle
- [ ] Please see me
- [ ] Please call back
- [ ] Please note & return

RE :

→

To quote Max Boyce –

'I was there!!'

Date : Time :

tour to Ayutthaya. When night descends the Italian restaurant and the barbecue on the large terrace will be fully booked as usual. The wind and the waves carry snatches of Thai music from the cultural show across the river, where the local cuisine is celebrated at the *Sala Rim Naam*.

Sometimes a famous face appears in the door. Some are recognised. Others leave us guessing: 'I know that face – who was it?'

Late at night the tunes of Eric's jazz band come through the closed

Afternoon tea *in the Author's Lounge. Behind the wall in the hotel's exclusive library time appears to stand still.*

doors of the Bamboo Bar. Here at the bar stories are circulated just as they were in the good old days although rarely now does the subject turn to shipping, rubber slumps and rice prices. Rarely somebody orders pink gins, stenghas or Anderson's Specials. Today tourists drink 'Spritzer', long drinks and beer, Mai Tais and Gin Slings. Their questions are different, too: 'When does the floating market open?', 'What time does the *Oriental Queen* leave in the morning?' and, inevitably: 'Do you know a good tailor?'

Before midnight the blind pianist Martin comes downstairs from *Le Normandie* where he plays during dinner hours. He is led in by friendly hands. Her Majesty Queen Sirikit has listened to his music and likeed it very much.

For us it is time to leave the Grand Old Lady. The luggage is on the way downstairs. Chaturong Siewsutha, the chief concierge and secret lord of the lobby, has everything under control. The car is booked and waiting. The boys line up around the boot and count the suitcases and *nécessaires*.

Good Likit Howsagul stands next to the luggage, unceasingly scribbling fine words in small letters on luggage tags which he then carefully attaches to the suitcases. He started working at The Oriental in 1972. With a huge smile he hands out more luggage tags, all inscribed with messages.

One reads:

'To business that we love we rise betime,
And go to't with delight.'
W Shakespeare (1564–1616)

Now the driver is ready. The farewell ceremony is in full swing. Hugs, goodbyes and promises to return soon. Sir Peter Ustinov's charming sentence springs to mind: 'When I leave I'll already be on my way back!'

Now the cream-white limousine glides through narrow lanes towards New Road making its way to the new highway.

The grand river, the mother of all waters, is left far behind. Spectators gather like every evening on the terrace of The Oriental. The lacy river has come to a standstill, performing its daily change of direction, as the water of the Gulf of Thailand now flows upstream. The first sun-downers are ordered while all eyes are riveted by the sight of the red fireball sinking majestically behind huge monsoon clouds which parade over the horizon like a herd of mighty white elephants.

Chaturong Siewsutha
lord of the lobby, welcomes a regular guest: Australian broadcaster and traveller **Rex Morgan.**
He, much to the surprise of all the staff, appeared in the uniform of his old regiment, the Legion of Frontiers, to attend the funeral of Her Majesty, the Queen Mother, in March 1996. Mr Morgan patronised the hotel for over 20 years, his guest record shows more than 100 visits. He is also a supporter of the SEA Write Award.

1876 1996

***Her Majesty, Queen Sirikit** of Thailand, honoured the concert of **José Carreras** with her presence. The Oriental's terrace was converted into a concert hall with 1.700 seats. This evening on 1 December 1996 marked the climax of year-long celebrations honouring the 50th anniversary of His Majesty's accession to the throne and of the hotel's 120th anniversary.*

*It all started with a grand party on 22 January 1996. From left host **Kurt Wachtveitl**, General Manager of The Oriental with **Khun Adisorn Charanachitta**, Director of The Oriental Hotel (Thailand) Public Co Ltd, The Governor of Bangkok, **Professor Krisda Arunwongse** and the Managing Director of the Mandarin Oriental group, **Robert E. Riley**.*

Almost a century has passed since the Oriental Hotel first opened its doors. During this time the Grand Old Lady of Bangkok, the Oriental, has played host to the legendary figures of the East. Kings and heads of state have walked her corridors, dined in her restaurants. From Somerset Maugham and Joseph Conrad, to Yehudi Menuhin and Danny Kaye, from Henry Ford II to James Michener and Noel Coward, from the Crown Prince of Norway to Mr. Edmund de Rothschild – the many guests who have stayed here have all fallen under the spell of this charming Old Lady.

First page of The Oriental's first golden guestbook

Elizabeth Taylor

WHO *was* THERE?

AN ATTEMPT AT AN ACCOUNT

Rarely do we find a hotel in the world that has a more extensive and impressive VIP guest list than The Oriental.

SIR PETER AND LADY USTINOV

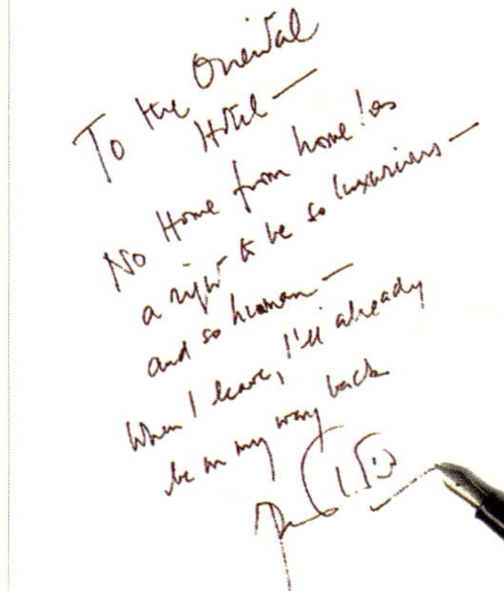

To the Oriental Hotel —
No Home from home! as a right to be so luxurious —
and so human —
When I leave, I'll already be on my way back

. . . When I leave I'll already be on my way back.

Jeffrey Archer signing in, former PR manageress Khun Pornsri and Khun Ankana are watching while Andrew Lloyd Webber is having a party with his wife.

Left: Sophia Loren, Gavin Young, Roger Moore, Julie Andrews, Lauren Bacall and son Robards, Kurt Wachtveitl welcomes Rajiv and Sonja Ghandi, Mick Jagger, Audrey Hepbrun with husband and David Rockefeller with his wife in the Somerset Maugham Suite.

Adjani Eric
Alexandre de Paris
Ambler John
Andrews Julie
Archer Jeffrey
Armstrong Neil
Arpels Mr&Mrs Philippe
Atkinson Kim
Attenborough, Sir Richard & L.
Aubert Jean-Claude
Aznavour Charles
Bacall Lauren & Robards
Baez Joan
Balestra Renato
Balmain Pierre
Barnard Christian Prof
Barnes Nick
Bartlett Hall
Baxter Anne
Beattie Anne
Becker Boris
Belmondo Jean Paul
Bhicharnchitr Worachai
Bisset Jaqueline
Bjornsdotter Cecilia
Blamey W S
Bocuse Paul
Bolshoi Theatre
Borg Björn
Boriboon Burin
Bouwer Sandra
Bowie David
Bradley Ed
Brannon Robert L
Brillantes G
Brosnan Pierce
Brogen Pierre
Bronfman E M Mr &Mrs
Brotherhood of Man
Buffet Bernard
Burns George
Caine Michael & Shakira
Cardin Pierre
Carey Peter
Carr Allan
Carreras José Maria
Carroll Diahann
Cartland Barbara
Chan Jackie
Charles Ray
Cimino Michael
Clement Richard
Coburn James
Colen D J
Conrad Joseph
Connery Sean
Cooper Edward jr
Corbett Ronnie
Cornwell David (John Le Carré)
Cousteau Jaques-Yves
Coward, Sir Noel,
Crawford Michael
Cronkite Walter, C B S
Cruise Tom
Dahl Arlene
Dajani A
De Niro Robert
De Voss David
Dench Dame Judi
Desavesa Chavane Choen
Devakul Tri M L
Dhammachoti Ussiri
Dillon Matt
Dior Christian
Diskul Galavanardis M C
Douglas Eric
Eastham Richard & Mrs
Eastwood Alison & Kyle
Eden Barbara
Estefan Gloria & family
Fairbanks Douglas Sr
Feibleman Peter
Ferry Brian
Field Sally
Finkbeiner-Zellmann Peter
Fisher Carrie
Fleming Alexander
Fleming Ian
Flick F K Dr
Flierbach H Rolf
Fluor Robert J &wife
Forbes Malcolm, Christopher
Ford Harrison
Forsyth Frederick
Fox Michael J
Gabor Eva
Gainsbourg Serge
Gangler Julie

The Oriental
Sports Centre
Openin anuary 1983
Borg

A connoisseur of the fairer sex Silvester Stallone seems to have had a good time at The Oriental while PR legend Khun Pornsri is successfully persuading David Bowie to authograph the guest book.

Left: Mel Gibson, Björn Borg, Bette Middler, David Puttnam, Pierce Brosnan, Ryan O'Neal, Gore Vidal, Pele, Arndt Krupp, Frederick Forsyth, Pierre Cardin.

Garret Leif
Gemma Giuliano
Gibson Mel
Giraudet Pierre
Glas Uschi
Godunov Alexander
Golding William & Anne
Gray Linda
Greene Graham
Guerlain Philippe
Guyer David
Hackman Gene
Hagman Larry
Hancock Herbie
Harrison George
Hawke Bob
Hawn Goldie
Hayden Bill
Heath B W
Henkel Gabriele
Henkel Konrad Dr
Hennessy Gilles
Hepburn Audrey
Heston Charlton
Hillary, Sir Edmund
Hitchock Alfred
Holmer E C
Hudson Ernie
Humperdinck Engelbert
Hutasing Toum
Jackson Michael
Jagger Mick
Jarre Jean-Michel
John Elton
Johnson Don
Kane Brian Dr
Kelly Grace
Kennedy D Mr&Mrs
Khoman Thanat Dr
King Alan
King Don
Kingston Maxine Hong
Kitt Eartha
Kostelanetz André
Kruger Hardy
Lacoste Bernard
Lamsam Bancha
Laube William T
Lauda Niki
Lauder Leonard
Laurent Yves St
Leach Robin
Lee Christopher
Lennox Anne
Levin Boris M
Linen James A III
Link Alma Khunying
Link G A Dr
Loren Sophia
Lowes Tony
Luce Boothe Clar
Ludwig Christa
MacNee Patrick
Mailer Norman
Marks Mary-Ellen
Marone Cinzano
Marriott III John Willard
Martin Mary
Matteson John R
Maugham Somerset
Mehta Zubin
Menuhin Yehudi
Michener James A
Midler Bette
Mills, Sir John
Mimieux Yvette
Mochtar Kusumaatwadja Prof Dr
Moore Roger
Moreno Rita
Mori Hanae
Moss Stirling
Mountbatten Leggy
Muldoon Robert
Naghaway I
Nakamura Mr
Nakasone Yashuhiro
Nakorn Na Saengdoen
Khunying
Nanabhiwat Boonying
Nandhabhiwat Sarapee
Khunying
Navaphan Sukhum
Navratilova Martina
Newhart Bob
Nicholson Jack
Nijinsky Waslav
Nilsson Birgit
Niro Robert de
Nureyev Rudolf

Happy moments at The Oriental for Michael and Shakira Caine and Gene Hackman's family

---

Ogilvy David
Palma Brian de
Papp Joseph
Parker Maynard
Parrot JeanMarie
Pelé (Edson Arantes do Nascimento)
Penn Sean
Philips Captain Mark
Piatelli Bruno
Poitier Sydney
Polanski Roman
Pongpaiboon Naowarat
Powell Jane
Powers Stephanie
Pramoj Kukrit
Pramoj Usni M L
Presley Priscilla
Price Vincent
Promphen Vilai
Prussia Lee

Barbara Cartland

Pulitzer Joseph III
Puttnam David
Rafelson Bob
Raffin Deborah
Rampling Charlotte
Rauschenberg Robert
Reagan Maureen
Rees Roger
Richard Pierre
Ross Diana
Roux Michel
Rowntree Richard
Sachs Gunter
Salikun Bin Mauri
Sarasin Pong
Sathienthai Surakiat
Sayer Leo
Schumacher Michael
Sedaka Neil
Selleck Tom
Sharif Omar
Sheldon Sidney & Jorja
Shelton Deborah
Shipley Walter
Smith Harold
Smith Wilbur
Squier Billy
Stallone Sylvester
Stamp Terence
Stanislaw James
Steinbeck John
Stewart Jackie and family
Stone Oliver
Straub Peter
Strauss Peter
Struthers Sally
Sukhanetr Sribhume
Sutherland Dame Joan
Suyin Han

Taittinger Virginia Dard
Takase Nagayuki
Tamchai Orasa, Dr
Taylor Elizabeth
Theroux Paul
Turner Tina
Ustinov, Sir Peter
Van Cleef & Arpels
Van Dame Jean Claude
Vanderbilt W C
Vidal Gore
Vine William
Viravaiday Marisa
Virawan Amnuay Dr
Voon Wong Meng Dr
Vuitton Louis
Wallace Mike
Warwick Dionne
Washam Joanne
Watanabe Sadao
Webber Sir Andrew L
West Morris
Williams Tennessee
Winter Roger
Wise Robert
Witt Hajo
Yanni John Christopher
Yevtushenko Yevgeniy
Yip Francis
Yipintsoi Misiem
Young Gavin
Young Paul

Royal, Noble and State Visits

Juan Carlos I, King of Spain, visited Bangkok and The Oriental with his charming wife, Queen Sofia. Her Majesty the Queen of England, Elizabeth II, arrived in Bangkok in 1996. The Oriental was the logical choice as Royal caterer for all Royal festivities. Later on HM thanked senior representatives of the staff for the exquisite food and service.

HIH The Crown Prince Naruhito and the Crown Princess Masako of Japan stayed at The Oriental during their visit to Bangkok. In 1980 Her Majesty Queen Sirikit presided over the SEA Write Award. Member of the jury James A Michener presented her with his latest work.

BANGKOK :: OCTOBER 1980
DURING A MOST DELIGHTFUL VISIT TO THE ORIENTAL AND TO THE SEAWRITE AWARDS. IT WAS FUN.

James A. Michener

The world of politics met in Bangkok for the Asian–European Meeting in 1996, bringing together Asian and European heads of states, in our pictures at a casual meeting at the hotel. Below some memories from the hotel's guest books: George Bush is welcomed by Kurt Wachtveitl in the traditional way with a flower garland, Margarete Thatcher arrives with her husband, Dr Mahatir of Malaysia received a true Oriental welcome with a flower carpet and Czech's Vaclav Havel arrives at the landing stage.

Akishino TIH Prince & Princess
Alahmadi Ali Muaaddi Aziz Abdul Bin Ahmed Prince
Albert Prince of Belgium
Alexander Prince of Belgium
Andreotti Giulio Prime Minister of Italy
Anne-Marie Queen of the Hellenes
Bedford Duke & Duchess
Bernhard Prince of the Netherlands
Bertil Prince of Sweden
Bhawani Maharaja of Jaipur
Bhirom Bhakdi Chamnong Khun
Birendra King of Nepal
Bismarck Barbara & Maximilian
Bongo El Hadj Omar Albert-Bernard of Gabun
Boutros Boutros-Ghali
Carl Gustaf XVI King of Sweden & Queen Silvia
Lord Carrington
Carter Rosalyn
Chand Kanidta
Chirac Jaques
Cinzano Count
Alberto & daughter
Constantine XI
Cuellar Perez
Dayan Moshe
Dini Lamberto
Diskul Subhadradis
Duke d'Antin
Duke of Edinburgh
Fuerstenberg George
von Prince &
Princess Victoria
Fuerstenberg Ira von
Fujimori Alberto President of Peru
Fukuda Takeo Prime Minister Japan
Gandhi Rajiv & Mrs Sonia Prime Minister of India
Genscher Hans Dietrich
George William Prince of Hanover
Goh Chok Tong & Mme Prime Minister of Signapore
Hassan al-Bolkiah Mu'izzad-din Waddaulah, Haji,
Sultan of Brunei
Havel Vaclav President
Hawke Bob Prime Minister Australia
Hawke J L Robert Australian PM
Heath Edward PM
Henrik Prince of Denmark
Hermannsson Steingrimurs P M of Scotland
Hitomi Hiroshi HE
Hohenzollern Dr.Johann George Prinz von
Hussein Abdullah Prince
Hussein TRH King of Jordan & Queen Noor
Ingrid Princess of DenmarkHE
Juliana Queen of the Netherlands
Keatin Paul Prime Minister of Australia
Kennedy David & wife
Ketudat Sippanondha Education Minister
Khoman Thanat Dr Deputy PM
Kissinger Henry Dr
Kittiyabha Bhajara Princess
Klestil Thomas President of Austria
Kohl Dr.Helmut & wife Hannelore
Krupp Annelise Baronin von Bohlen und Halbach
Krupp Arndt VI Baron von Bohlen und Halbach
Ladawan Thawisan M.L.
Lee Yew Kuan Prime MinisterSignapore & Mme
Lilian Princess of Sweden
Lusinan Jaime President of Venezuela
Margarethe II Queen of Denmark
Margarita Queen of Bulgaria
Masako HIH The Crown Princess of Japan
Michael Prince of Kent
Mohamad Datuk Seri Mahathir P M of Malaysia
Naruhito HIH The Crown Prince of Japan
Nixon Richard President USA
Noor Queen
Paduka Seri Sultan Azlan Muhibbuddin Shah Ibni
Almarhum Sultan Yussuf Izzuddin Ghafarullahu
Lahu Shah King of Malaysia
Papandreou Andreas Prime Minister of Greece
Pignatelli Luciana Princess
Prince of Wales and wife
Quayle Dan & Mrs US Vice President
Rainier III de Grimaldi Prince of Monaco
Ramos Fidel V, President Philippines
Reagan Nancy
Rocard Michel Prime Minister of France & Mme
Rockefeller David Mr & Mrs
Rojanastien Boonchu Deputy PM
Rojanastien Boonchu Deputy Prime ministerThailand
Rothschild Philippine de Baroness
Saad Al Abdullah Al Salim Al Sabah,
Crown Prince & Prime Minister of Kuwait
Sarasin Pote Prime Minister of Thailand
Sartzetakis Christos A President of Greece
Schlueter Poul Prime Minister of Danmark & wife
Schmidt Helmut
Shultz George
Shah Azlan Sultan
Shawcross Lord Hartley
Sihanouk Norodom Prince
Silvia Queen of Sweden
Simeon II King of Bulgaria
Sirikit Queen of Thailand
Sirindhorn Chakri Maha Princess
Soamsawali Princess
Soeharto Tojib N J President of Indonsia
Sofia R Queen of Spain
Sonja Princess of Norway
Spencer Earl & Lady Spencer
Stanislaw Mary-Anne
Sukarno Dewi
Suzuki Zenko Prime Minister of Japan & Mme
Talal Bin Mohammed Prince of Jordan
Talal M Prince of Jordan
Thatcher Margaret Lady Prime Minister & Denis
Thyssen-Bornemisza De Kaszon Hans Heinrich Baron
Trudeau Pierre Elliott
Vadhana Galyani Princess
Vranitzky Franz Chancellor Austria
Weinberger Caspar
Weizsäcker Richard Dr Federal President of Germany
& Marianne v.
Withayanand Waree
Yevtushenko Yevgeniy

From the hotel's collection

Let's meet at The Oriental

For over 120 years the hotel has been the meeting point in Bangkok and for discerning travellers it always was the meeting point in Thailand. Is Mr and Mrs so-and-so there? one asks upon arriving, swiftly proceeding through the lobby to the terrace where everybody always was and still is sitting to see and to be seen.

SELECTED BIBLIOGRAPHY

1,800 miles on a Burmese tat; Lt G J Younghusband, 1888

Andersen, Hans Niels; *Danish National Biography entry*, 1979

Around the world with General Grant (2 vols); John Russell Young, 1879

Around Tonkin and Siam; Prince Henry d'Orleans, 1894

Baedeker's *Indien*, 1914

Bangkok!; Frederick King Poole, 1970

Bangkok; James Kirkup, 1968

Bangkok Calendar; Dan Beach Bradley, 1859/60

Bangkok: its life and sport; Lt-Colonel C H Forty, 1929

Bangkok: portrait of a city; Philip Ward, 1974

Bangkok: Siam's city of angels; Germaine Krull, with Dorothea Melchers, 1964

Bangkok: the story of a city; Alec Waugh, 1970

Bangkok Waterways, An Explorer's Handbook, William Warren, R Ian Lloyd, 1989

Beyond the blue horizon; Alexander Frater, 1986

Commercial directory for Thailand, 1961–62

Consul in paradise; W A R Wood, 1965

The Directory for Bangkok and Siam, 1891 & 1894

East for pleasure; Walter B Harris, 1929

The English Governess at the Siamese court; Anna Leonowens, 1870

Engraved gems: their history and an elaborate view of their place in art; Maxwell Sommerville, 1889

Five years in Siam; H Warrington Smyth, 1898

Friendly Siam; Ebbe Kornerup, 1928

From Golden Gate to golden sun; Herman Norden, 1923

The Gentleman in the Parlour; W Somerset Maugham, 1930

Giorgio Berlingieri, 'His Book', Bangkok, 1982

Guide to Bangkok, Major Erik Seidenfaden 1927 (1st edition) & 1932 (3rd edition);

Guide to Bangkok; Margaretta B Wells, 1961

Guide to Thailand, land of smiles; 1968

Guidebook to Bangkok and Siam; J Antonis, 1904

A history of South-East Asia; D G E Hall, 1981

The Imperial, The first 100 Years of a Grand Hotel in Japan, Tokyo 1990

Imperial air routes; A E W Salt, 1930

Imperial Airways; N C Baldwin, 1950

In Search of Conrad, Gavin Young, 1991

Joseph Conrad: a biography; Roger Tennant, 1981

Joseph Conrad: the three lives; Frederick R Karl, 1979

Journey around myself; Felix Marti-Ibanez, 1966

Land of the moon flower; Gerald Sparrow, 1955

The land of the white elephant; Frank Vincent Jun, 1873

Louis and the King of Siam; W S Brostowe, 1976

Malayan symphony; W Robert Foran, 1935

Maugham: a reappraisal; John Whitehead, 1987

A new guide to Bangkok; Kim Korwong, 2nd edition 1950

An Oriental Album; presented by Giorgio Berlingieri

A padre in partibus; Rev George Reith, 1897

The Rich; William Davis, 1982

The romance of the harem; Anna Leonowens, 1873

Peter Karl Faberge: goldsmith and jeweller to the Russian Imperial Court; Henry Charles Bainbridge, 1949

Siam (2 volumes); W A Graham, 2nd edition 1924

Siam and Cambodia in pen and pastel; Rachel Wheatcroft, 1928

Siam and China; Salvatore Besso (translated by C Matthews), 1914

Siam basic handbook, 1945

Siam das Reich des Weissen Elefanten; Ernst von Hesse-Wartegg, 1899

The Siam Directory, 1958–59

Siam in the XXth century; J G D Campbell, 1902

Siam on the Meinam; Maxwell Sommerville, 1897

Siam (or the heart of farther India); Mary Lovina Cort, 1886

The Singapore and Straits Directory, 1887

The Singapore Treasury; Andreas Augustin, 1987

Temples and elephants; Carl Bock, 1884

The Times newspaper, 3 January 1937

Through the buffer state; J Macgregor, 1896

To Siam and Malaya in the Duke of Sutherland's yacht 'Sans Peur'; Mrs Florence Candy, 1889

Twentieth century impressions of Siam,1908

A vagabond in Asia; Edmund Chandler, 1900

Zig-zag journeys in the antipodes, 1888

THAILAND

Thailand, covering an area of 513,000 square kilometres (Great Britain is 245,000 sq kms, for example), lies in the heart of Southeast Asia, roughly equidistant between India and China.

It shares borders with Burma to the west and north, Laos to the north-east, Kampuchea to the east and Malaysia to the south. In topographical respect the country is divided into four distinct areas: the mountainous north, the fertile central plains, the semi-arid plateau of the northeast, and the peninsula south distinguished by its many beautiful tropical beaches and offshore islands.

Thailand has a population of about 53 million. Ethnic Thais form the majority, though the area has historically been a migratory cross-roads, and thus strains of Mon, Khmer, Burmese, Lao, Malay, Indian and, most strongly, Chinese stock produce a degree of ethnic diversity. Integration is such, however, that culturally and socially there is enormous unity.

Thailand celebrated the longest reign of all living monarchs in 1996. It has often been said that, apart from the normal economic and security requirements, the independence and integrity of Thailand are assured by three unifying factors: its people's freedom-loving spirit, the Buddhist Religion and the Thai Throne. Indeed, the three factors were already there at

the first founding of the first integrated Thai nation with its capital at Sukhothai more than seven centuries ago and have successfully survived the test of time just as Thailand itself has also survived as a united and independent country throughout its long history up to the present days.

T*hailand is a constitutional monarchy. Since 1932, Thai kings, including the present monarch, HM King Bhumibol Adulyadej, have exercised their legislative powers through a national assembly, their executive powers through a cabinet headed by a prime minister, and their judicial powers through the law courts.*

T*hailand's national religion is Theravada Buddhism, practised by more than 90 per cent of all Thais. The remainder of the population adheres to Muslim, Christian, Hindu and other faiths, all of which are allowed full freedom of expression. Buddhism continues to cast a strong influence on daily life.*

T*hailand has a yearly arrival of approximately seven million tourists thus making tourism a major source of the gross national product.*

T*hailand enjoys a healthy future. Its economy was projected by the World Bank to be ranked amongst the world top 10 by the year 2010.*

T*hailand is the home of a hotel situated along the 'King of the Rivers', the 'Mother of all Waters', the Chao Phraya River. It is called The Oriental and it stands in the heart of the capital Bangkok for over 120 years, a grand testimony of Thai welcome and world class hospitality.*